# SOUTHERN

# CALIFORNIA'S

# BEST

# SURF

# SOUTHERN CALIFORNIA'S BEST SURF

A Guide to Finding, Predicting,
and Understanding the Surf
of Southern California

by

Tom Wegener
Bill Burke

Green Room Press
P. O. Box 7000-691
Redondo Beach, California 90277

15th St. Del Mar. Photo Matt LaZich

Cover by Wendy Price.

Sketches by Brett Dean, Pgs. 3, 13, 17, 29, 38, 40, 53, 62, and 93.

Type setting by Stiles Wegener.

Satellite photos by NASA.

Special thanks to Stiles Wegener and David Lane for editing, proofreading, and advice. Also, mil gracias (thanks) to everyone who helpd by donating photos, stories, and constructive criticism.

Mark Sharp on a fun little California shoulder, above. Photo Matt LaZich. Below, two men drop into a not so fun California giant.

# Table of Contents

Brett Dean, artist of this book, finds his own smooth, wedging peak.

# Introduction to Surfology

## (the study of good surf)

It has been said many times, possibly too many, that you can't fool mother nature. This is true, but when it comes to surf prediction, there is a great deal to be learned, and with this information you can learn to predict its behavior. This book gives the basics for understanding the surf and why it is good at some breaks during certain conditions and not at others. In addition, it explains how waves are formed and how to predict their arrival at the Southern California coast. With this information the surfer is better prepared to predict and find good surf, thus becoming much more in tune with the ocean.

The practices and guidelines of this book are instinctive to most highly experienced surfers. Everyone knows at least one person who is always on top of it when the surf is good, even though that person is just as busy as the rest of us. The chances are that he doesn't merely have good luck. Rather, he possesses a fine understanding of the variables which make good surf so that he knows when and where it will be best. This book gives you the tools for understanding and predicting waves. But the tools alone are only a part of understanding the surf variables. You also need to add dedication and experience to this study of surfology so you can see for yourself how all the elements of the surf work together. With some time and effort you can be that person who always seems to be on the surf when it's best.

The contents of the following pages are the result of the authors' perpetual search for good surf, utilizing theory and experience. The guidelines are generally based on scientific knowledge of waves. But due to the extreme number of variables involved in understanding and predicting surf (i.e. swell direction, wind force, wave size), predictions based on the information in this book cannot be super-precise. You are never positive how the surf will be two blocks or five counties away, or two days into the future. For example, theory suggests that if you had all of the necessary wind velocities of a storm and the distance of water that the high winds covered, you could precisely predict the size of the swells that would be produced. Unfortunately, this precise swell prediction is rather unattainable for almost all surfologists because it is impossible to get the measurements needed for accurate predictions. Winds are usually measured by various ships which are out at sea. But the middle of a storm is probably the last place in the world you would ever find a ship. And when ships are caught in big storms, the crew is usually battening down the hatches, praying, and wondering why they did not become barbers, not measuring the wind velocities. Thus, as surf predictors, we don't have access to all of the infor-

mation needed for perfect surf predictions. Due to the lack of infor-mation, surf predicting is not a totally precise science. We can't make hard, math-based calculations because we lack precise numbers and conse-quently often rely on hunches, instinct, and induction. Surf finding is more of a knack, like cooking. Like a cook, the good surf predictor who has collected many pieces of knowledge about the swells, storms, winds, and tides can piece them together to see where the tastiest spot will be. But he is never actually sure how his meal will taste before he takes his first bite.

There are as many kinds of surfers in Southern California as there are people. For example, the categories include pros, longboarders, longboard kooks, knee boarders, boogie boarders, ultra-light riders, surf posers, gyro wankers... but whatever the category, there will always be the dedicated sur-fer. An individual truly dedicated to surfing pursues his sport regardless of the external forces surrounding the rest of his life. The pursuit of quality surf can be done on a global level, as is well known; however, on a day-to-day basis, a true surfer focuses his attention locally. Most surfers have a favorite spot, but the best surfers are flexible. The idea of flexibility will be a prime focus in this book, for each spot is different and comes alive under its own conditions. The wise surfer, with his vast knowledge of many locations, will always attempt to hit the best one around, not im-mediately run to his favorite spot. As was said in Bruce Brown's classic film Endless Summer, "Size isn't the most important element in good surf; quality is." To consistently find quality surf, you must be flexible and knowledgeable enough to be able to show up at the right spot at the right time.

This book uses many well-known surf spots as examples to illustrate how the surf variables can come together to create good waves. The locals at these spots probably won't be too thrilled with this because they don't want everyone to show up at their spot when all of the proper conditions come together. The point of the examples is to get the reader to look at his own stomping grounds and to find breaks which are similar to these examples, not to visit the spots cited. The goal is to help people get "dialed in" to their own spots, so they know when and where the surf will be good.

The authors also advocate traveling to new spots, especially since many people live in areas which are flat during certain swells. Instead of making the best of a hopeless situation, we recommend that you travel to places where it's good. But we beg the traveler to be cool and to remember your basic purpose. The goal is to have fun, to relax, hang out... essentially to surf. The right thing to do is to treat others, when at their spots, the way you think they should act toward you. Give them some respect, and instead of showing how rad you are, check out how their styles have conformed to their local surf conditions.

Chris Olivas cuts back at Pt. Dume.

A guy missing a perfect slider at Torrance Beach, winter of 1982.

Cardiff Reef: with a strong understanding of many spots, not just a few, the smart surfer will always be able to avoid the vicious crowds, or at least he will be able to make the best of conditions.

Author Tom Wegener shown here making the best of a mediocre day at Haggerty's.

A clean north swell at Cardiff Reef. Note the long line on the swell which is characteristic of Cardiff during north swells.

Tabletops: one of San Diego's most finicky spots that breaks only on the deepest of south swells.

Here is Stewart being scared on a big wave in Northern California.

The worst threat to surfing is not overcrowding but bad attitudes. Be reasonable when considering where to surf. Sometimes a break is so crowded that you have no business paddling out. Sometimes it's best to wait for the crowd to thin out or to just simply go somewhere else. The coast is absolutely loaded with spots. Most are not Rincons or Malibus, but they still are excellent places to surf when the conditions are right. Furthermore, there is seldom a crowd at the "out-of-the-way" spots, and the material in this book can help you come to know these areas. The authors have lived in quite a few different places, but no matter where we have spent time, we have always been able to find many "backyard" spots which are occasionally phenomenal and never crowded. This book gives the basics for predicting how the surf will be in the future so you can plan ahead and be one of the first people on the swell.

# Part I: General Concepts of Surf and the Elements of Finding Good Surf

## Swell Direction

Knowledge of the swell direction is probably the most important element in seeking out good surf, and it is usually the first thing to check when contemplating where to surf. Most breaks are affected in some way by the swell direction; that is, they break differently with different swells. For example, Cardiff reef will break on any swell, but it peels and has more bowls when the swell is more out of the north. Most of the southern California beaches break good on deep souths, while they usually close out on big lined up wests. Some places are completely missed by swells from the wrong direction. For example, Malibu may be a lake while just around the corner Zuma and County Line may be pumping. Always remember that every spot is different; if you know how each spot reacts to the different wave directions, you can better decide where the surf will be best on any given day.

In California, surfers generally recognize three directions from which the swells come: north, west, and south. But in actuality, these names for the swell directions are not really accurate due to the positioning of California. Southern California generally faces southwest, but when we stand on the beach and look straight out, we envision ourselves facing west. And when a lined up swell comes in which is perfectly parallel to the beach, we say it is out of the west, even though it is really out of the south-west. In the same way, what surfers call north swells are really out of the west, while souths can come up from the south-east. (Furthermore, there are very seldom swells from due east.) But, one major problem is that meteorologists

8

are more inclined to speak of swells out of their true directions, so when they say that a west swell is running, we must interpret it as a north-west swell in order to envision how it will hit the local beaches. Generally, what people mean by a north swell is a real issue in surfology. In this book we will continue the surfer tradition by sticking to the less accurate titles.

Sometimes two or more swells come in from different directions at the same time. Though this often occurs, it can be difficult to detect. This condition usually creates clean peaks which quickly back off in one direction and slowly peel in the other. A friend of ours, Stewart Sweeney, was once at a left point break in Northern California when a big north and a big southwest were arriving at the same time. He said that some sets would come out of the south and mix with the smaller waves between the sets out of the north, breaking in a rather powerless, mushy fashion down the point. But when the sets out of the north mixed with the smaller waves out the south, they peeled down the point. When a set out of the north came in at the same time as a set out of the south, there were huge, powerful peaks which scared Stewart and which ended up breaking down the point just like a regular set out of the north.

## Detecting Swell Direction

The best way to check the swell direction is to actually go down to the water's edge and look at the waves. Look up or down the coast and try to see if the waves are breaking towards or away from you. If the waves are breaking towards you, that is the direction from which the swell is coming. Generally, the direction from which you see more peeling waves is the direction out of which the surf is coming. Of course, on many days, the surf is out of the west and the waves are hitting the beach evenly; in other words, the swells are coming in parallel to the shore. Often the beaches are walled out at these times.

The direction the beach or reef face is always a factor because it may give tainted information about the swell. For example, if the beach is facing south, a west swell may appear to be out of the north. Once again, some experience and thinking about the local breaks is needed in order to understand what is going on. The better understanding one has of his local area, the more accurately he will be able to the predict surf conditions in his own turf as well as in other areas.

At most point breaks and some reef breaks, the swell direction is not easily detectable. The different depths and bottom formations can switch the waves around so that, without a good deal of experience, one would have some difficulty seeing which way the swells were coming from. Another way to find the swell direction is by reading the weather page in

When you are in Santa Barbara, looking straight out to sea, you are looking due south.

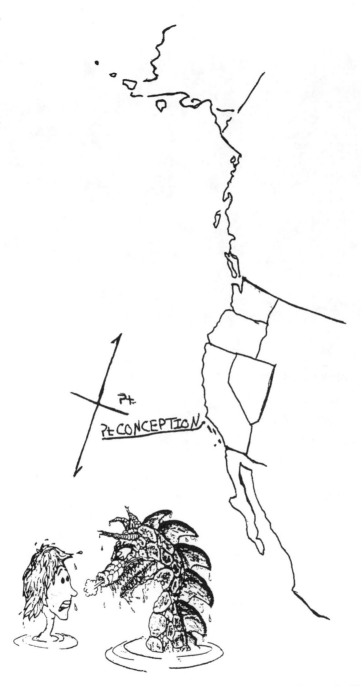

Swells out of the true north pass right by us in Southern California because our coast faces southwest. What we call "north" swells are really more out of the west.

Guy Trotter floats across a closed out wall.  Photo Matt LaZich.

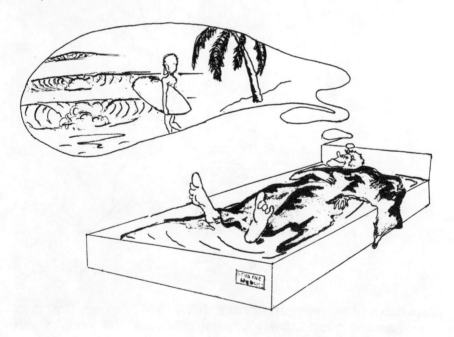

Author, Tom Wegener, sits poised on the nose while contemplating metaphysical issues. Carlsbad, winter of 1986.

South swells lazily roll up the coast.

Slade Fester takes off on one of the biggest waves of the year.
Lunada Bay, Feb. I, 1986. Photo Tom Good.

Todos Santos.     Photo by Gary Baldwin. Note Todos Santos'
positioning on the map

Mike deNicola at Churches, I/89, USA National Team Member.

Author Bill Burke shown here on a crispy winter evening at his favorite reef break. This spot breaks only on a north swell at low tide.

the paper or by listening to the marine weather channel. The radio is very accurate and can sometimes give information about the swell which one could not see when looking at the surf. Many times the authors have missed excellent surf because they checked Torrance beach (northwest facing) in the morning and saw that it was very small. We thought that there was nothing out there at all. But at the same time Malibu (30 miles north) was six feet. If we had checked the marine channel, it probably would have informed us that there was a large swell from the south.

The weather page's forecast for the swell direction is reasonably accurate, but it always seems to be a day or so behind. Thus, if you want to know yesterday's swell direction, then the place to check would be the newspaper. We think the reason for this is first, the swell direction usually stays out of the same direction for a few days. Therefore, when they make the forecast, they merely look at what the weather service gave as the swell direction for the previous day. Second, the swell direction is a very difficult thing to predict, especially over large areas of water, and it is even more difficult when there is more than one swell running at one time. Third, very few people who read the paper really care if this information is accurate.

## Biggest Where Facing Into Swell

One of the few rules of wave prediction is that the waves are always biggest in places where the coast faces into the swell. On many days one is desperately searching for a place that is big enough to have even the potential for good surf. As the swells roll along the coast, they come upon many different places which face a variety of directions. When they break at places where they come in at an angle, their size and breaking power is smaller because their power is concentrated over a long breaking line. When the waves hit a place which faces into the swell direction, they achieve their maximum size and power. For example, a truck will hit a wall of bricks harder if it runs straight into it than it would if it struck it at an angle.

You can see how the surf size changes as the direction of the coast changes on almost any day when you travel more than fifty miles along the coast. Most surfers have observed this many times. Not long ago one of the authors made an early morning surf check in Carlsbad (southwest facing), finding it very small and out of the north. Lacking surf gumption, I crept back into bed to dream of good surf (sleeping on water beds is truly conducive to surfing dreams). A few hours later I had to drive to Point Loma, about an hour south. On the way I passed Cardif reef (west facing), which was about head high and fun looking. Driving a little faster now, I made it down to Point Loma and Sunset Cliffs (west facing but very open to north swells) to see double overhead swells pumping in. I took care of my business with haste and sped back to Carlsbad, thinking that the surf was picking up.

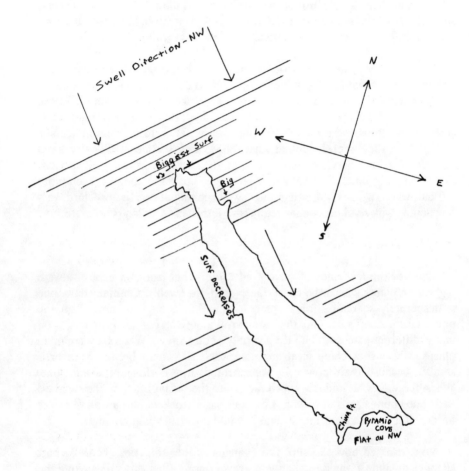

Surf biggest where facing into swell; e.g. San Clemente Island.

But I only found the same waste high dribbling mush that was there in the morning. This event pointed out to me, for the one thousandth time, the importance of going to the areas which face into the swell.

Islands are unquestionably the best place to look for big surf, for some part always points straight into the swell. For example, the island of Todos Santos in Northern Mexico is becoming famous for its large surf. Often the beaches on the mainland will be small, while the island is getting pounded.

San Clemente Island, around fifty miles west of Newport Beach, sees a lot of big waves. During the big swells of 1983, Captain Curt Wegener (the brother of one of the authors) was out near the north end of San Clemente where the swells were directly hitting the island. He told me that the waves were so big that nobody could put a number on them, but they could tell that they were fully breaking in over 50 feet of water. The mainland had surf up to thirty-five feet high, but it is debatable whether this surf ever broke in over 25 feet of water.

## Swells Get Smaller as They Break Down a Point

A corollary to the last rule is that waves get smaller and usually cleaner as they roll down into a bay or down a long point. This is good to know for the beginning surfer, who may not have the desire to paddle out into large surf. Also, it is essential for finding a good place to surf when the swell is very choppy.

When traveling Baja one of the factors you have to contend with is the mean north winds which seem to blow almost all day and chop up the surf. Fortunately, there are quite a number of points which face south. At these places, the north wind blows straight offshore, and the swells clean up because they have to bend all the way around the point.

There are a few points like this in Santa Barbara. Probably the most well-known is Campus Point, which is almost on the U.C. Santa Barbara campus. Often large choppy swells which are difficult to surf move down from Point Conception, but after they wrap around Campus Point, they're much cleaner and definitely more surfable.

Up in Northern California, where the sea is rough and the winds blow out of the north most of the time, the knowledge of points and bays is especially important. Once when traveling around the Humboldt area, one of the authors was amazed to find the Mendocino Beach break clean with a nice offshore wind, while just outside the point it was literally "victory at sea." (This term is derived from the old war movies which always opened up with a battleship pounding through some very mean seas.)

Punta Santa Rosilita, one of the many endless point breaks in Baja. This point faces perfectly south, and on this day the surf was out of the north. The swell was actually bumpy at north facing beaches, but it cleaned up and becames smaller as it bent around the point.

This photo of San Augustine's in Santa Barbara County is a prime example of how swell direction can be difficult to determine due to reef configuration.

This clean Carlsbad peeler is the product of a lined up south mixed with a choppy northwest.

Cherry Street in Carlsbad, one of the places in San Diego where the south swells come in straight on. When there is any kind of south running, it is always one of the biggest and most consistent spots.

Mysto right, Southern California, winter of 1983. Many spots that seldom break came alive with the giant El Nino winter of 1983. Many waves went unridden.

One time one of the authors was on a fishing boat off San Clemente Island when I saw the most unusual break I have ever encountered. A hundred or so yards off the island was a smaller island which was about the size of a football field. The swell that day was about 15 feet high and very bumpy. The waves would begin breaking at the northernmost tip of the island and break all the way around it until the wave smashed into itself on the other side. As the wave wrapped around the island, it transformed from a bumpy, hard-to-surf wave to a clean peeler. When the wave first broke, it was sloppy and bumpy. But as it passed by the spot where I was anchored, the swells began to line up or get longer, and they appeared to be breaking in shallower water because they formed large spinning tubes. As the waves rolled away from me, they appeared to be only shoulder high, but they had cleaned up and the bump was gone. They were now peeling perfectly. When you are fishing and not looking for good waves, you will often come into situations where you would happily trade all your fish to surf.

## Swell Windows

Some places are very sensitive to swell direction due to their location. Islands, points, and peninsulas may block certain swells from reaching specific areas. The swell window of a break is the direction from which surf can come and reach the shore with the majority of its original strength. For example, Malibu's swell window faces from south to west.

Learning how to surf in Palos Verdes, the authors once thought that south swells were weak and seldom overhead. This belief is not surprising due to the fact that Catalina serves effectively as a 26 mile long breakwater which almost completely blocks south breaks. Palos Verdes has a swell window open only to norths and wests. It was on my first trip to Newport Beach on a big south that I became brutally enlightened to the true size and potential power of south swells.

Santa Barbara has an acute swell window due to the positioning of Santa Rosa, Santa Cruz, and San Miguel islands. Its window is open to norths and wests, while south swells are blocked by the islands. Thus, Santa Barbara surfers must either surf those islands which block the waves or travel up or down the coast in order to surf south swells to their full potential.

Southern California is sheltered by Point Conception. Many high winds and rough seas miss us because we are in the lee of the point. For example, any fishing boat captain will tell you that there is a big difference between the average weather conditions at Morro Bay harbor and Newport Beach harbor. Generally, Southern California has an open window to some of the

Mike deNicola shralps a small clean wave at Cottons on a north swell.

Big Rock is open to almost all swells.

Bill Burke gets covered at the Hollister ranch by a south swell which barely made it around the Channel Islands.

Indonesia comes to Paddleboard Cove.

Jon Wegener drops in on a west swell at Storks, which faces west.

Happy grommet cuts back at La Jolla.

swells and weather which come down the coast, but if you venture 60 miles out to sea, you will find yourself out of the lee of Point Conception and into the rough ocean. Sometimes when you are wondering if life could get any worse, listen to the marine weather channel and be happy that you are not in a leaky boat 80 miles out.

## Philosophy of Equipment Choice: Certain Boards and Styles are Best Fit for Individual Conditions

The gumptionful surfer, who is dedicated to getting the most out of the surf, usually is familiar with a wide variety of boards and styles. There are specialized boards and styles for the many different types of surf one may encounter. For example, most people would argue that a thruster or a short board is the best tool for riding steep, head-high peaks, though most boards would work in these waves. Also, nobody would argue that longboards are not the call for small mushy surf. Furthermore, big long pintails are best for triple overhead and up surf.

The surf changes from hour to hour and from day to day. The person who believes that the surf is always good somewhere close by (which is true) will have a much easier time being satisfied if he has the proper equipment and styles for all the different types of surf and conditions. Some people say that small thrusters are the only good surfboards, or at least the best, and everyone who knows what's up only rides them. This attitude is just as ridiculous as believing that there is only one good type of golf club, the 7 iron. The surfer most in tune with the surf is ready for any set of conditions. Furthermore, of the great surfers I have come to know, most of them agree that having experience with many types of surfing greatly enhances their own style overall.

Many times I have gone to Mexico with big dreams of finding huge, gnarly, perfect waves. Thus, in preparation I always bring some of the most up-to-date equipment to shred my dream waves. Unfortunately, however, I am what is known as a black cloud. Almost every time I've been exploring in Mexico, I have experienced one of those rare, lengthy flat spells. Anticipating less than perfect surf, I always bring an old longboard and a boogie board. As it turns out, I have spent most of my Mexico hours longboarding what little surf I could find. "What a pain in the behind that longboard must be to drag around," people often say when they see me traveling with it. But they don't understand that old longboards have many uses other than surfing. For example, they make good tables, fishing barges, boards for other people to borrow, and traction boards to put under your tires when you are stuck in the sand.

## Waves Feel the Bottom

The energy of a swell stretches one half the wave's length beneath the surface, and this lower energy of the swell is what encounters the bottom and eventually causes the wave to break. In the open ocean the waves travel at full speed because they encounter little friction from the sea floor. As the water becomes shallower, they begin to slow down because the swell starts to drag along the bottom. This friction with the bottom causes the wave to become steeper and eventually break. Essentially, the front of the wave moves more slowly than its back, which causes the whole thing to topple over itself.

Powerful waves are generally formed when the swells come straight out of the deep water and don't lose energy to bottom drag. Mushy, powerless waves travel over greater distances of shallow water before breaking.

## Effects of the Various Bottom Formations on the Surf

The sea floor has a tremendous effect on the waves and how they break. The rule is that the swells move slower when in shallower water; that is, the waves slow when the depth is less than half their wave length. Often there are varying depths just outside the surf break which can affect the swells by slowing and deforming parts of them.

Undersea canyons are a graphic example of this. The part of the wave which comes in over the canyon moves at full speed when nearing the beach, while the part of the swell which is over the shallower fringes of the canyon slows down. This creates a bend in the swell, which is called a "bowl." This bowl or pocket in the swell has a profound effect on the wave as it is breaking. Generally a large peak is formed at the bowl which is larger than the original swell, and the wave peels off in both directions from the center of the peak (providing the proper conditions are found, namely, a relatively even depth around the breaking zone). But in order for the bowl effect to take place, the swell must be lined up or long enough to stretch from the shallow areas to the deeper waters. Basically, the energy of the part of the swell which passed over the canyon is sucked into the peak. Though the bowl effect is most pronounced where undersea canyons meet the shore, it also occurs at most point and reef breaks. A reef far outside of the impact zone can begin forming the swell into a peel long before the wave actually breaks. Watching swells deform from the different ocean floor depths is really quite interesting, especially when you can get a good aerial view of a break.

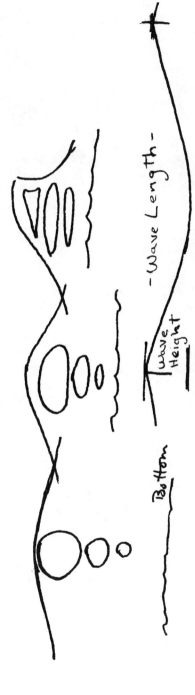

The circles and ovals represent the water movement as the wave passes. As the wave comes into shallower water, the bottom of the wave begins to feel the bottom, causing the wave to get taller, and the front goes slower than the back.

WAVE LENGTH   Wave length is measured in seconds: the time it takes for one trough to pass a given point such as a buoy.

31

Black's Beach. Note how these double overhead sets out of the north refract due to the canyon.

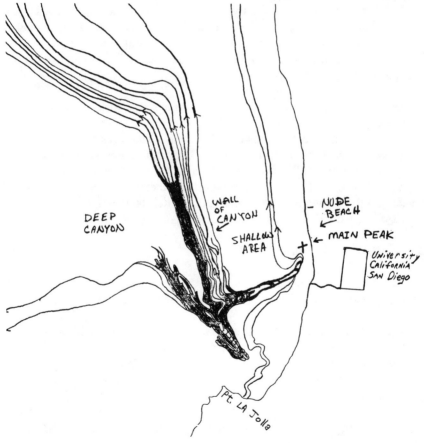

The canyon at Black's Beach. The deep canyon comes within a seven iron shot from the beach. This causes the waves to bend, forming large bowls and peaks.

Some breaks are a combination of beach and reef. Reefs which stick up from a normally sandy bottom often form some unexpected boils and mean sections. For example, one of the authors once experienced this condition when surfing Black Beach in Northern California. I would casually take off on a mellow peak, thinking that the wave was going to be clean and easy. Suddenly the bottom would "drop out" because of a shallow reef, and a huge tube would take the place of the fluffy shoulder.

## Sucking In Swells

Sometimes a break seems to be larger than all the other spots in the area for no apparent reason. There is a relatively straight stretch of beach which should have the same size surf all the way down, but instead one or two spots are obviously bigger or more consistent than the rest. For example, on some south swell days you can drive along the North San Diego County coast and see the same size surf for miles, but upon reaching Tamarack, you may see surf which is a little larger and more consistent than usual. (Unfortunately, the crowd there is consistently much larger than that of the other near-by spots.)

The authors are not absolutely sure why some spots suck in the surf, but the theory seems to be that just outside of the break there is a high spot or shallow area which creates a bowl in the swell. This makes the waves larger and causes them to break further out. Also, this can make a break more consistent because swells which would have broken a little bigger further down the beach, if the high spot were not there, may have their energy concentrated to the area of the high spot. When searching for good surf it is always a good idea to keep an eye out for spots which suck in the swells.

## The Different Types of Swells

There is a fundamental difference between peaky, short intervaled swells (wind swells) and lined up, long intervaled swells (ground swells).

Peaky wind swells break best at beaches because the swell itself is already shaped into a peak, and when it hits an even bottom, it breaks with good shape all by itself. Most coastal areas in California have nice flat beaches, and there is lots of room for surfers to get good waves during wind swells. The main problem with surfing wind swells is that it can be difficult to paddle out when the surf is overhead. The waves are so close together that the surfer receives an almost constant pounding while paddling out.

Youngster enjoys a clean day at Sunset Cliffs.

Tamarack: A prime recipient for south swells.

Brett Dean, riding a wave which is heavily deformed by an uneven bottom. It is only 14 inches deep over the table reef where he is riding, but it is even shallower down the line where the front of the wave has already broken before the back of the wave has hit the shelf. Note how stoked Sean Turner is as he stands over a little bit deeper section of the reef.

Wind swells usually don't work very well at reef and point breaks because they are not influenced much by the bottom formations. Since these waves have shorter intervals, they do not feel the bottom until they are in relatively shallow water. Thus, a bowl has less of a chance to form. In addition, wind swells don't usually stretch from the shallow water to the deep water. This cuts down the possibility of a bowl forming, and it keeps the wave from breaking evenly down a long reef or point.

## Ground Swells

Ground swells are caused by storms far off coast. The further away the waves are formed, the more lined up and distanced they will be from each other. As swells travel away from the high winds of the storm which created them, they slowly merge together and clean up to form long lines, and the distance between the swells increases (longer interval). Thus, from a wind swell a ground swell is formed, but it takes a great distance for the clean-up process to occur. For example, New Zealand swells are created the greatest distance from us, and they are the most lined up, with intervals of up to twenty-four seconds. Regular Cabo San Lucas souths and distant northwests are also lined up and clean, but not so much so as the New Zealands. Wind swells which are created just off the coast of California are a mess (short intervaled and not lined up).

Once during Christmas vacation, the news media carried many stories and shots of a giant storm surf off San Francisco. The next day Southern California experienced some triple overhead surf which was fairly clean, but still had short intervals and some bumps. About three days later one of the author's brothers witnessed some absolutely humungas and perfectly clean surf coming into the west-facing beaches of Cabo San Lucas. Theory has it that we got some of the large surf from the storm, but it was much bigger outside of the lee of Pt. Conception. As the swells moved south they cleaned up, and upon hitting the beaches of Cabo San Lucas, which are open to Norths, they exploded with their utmost power.

Ground swells break best at reefs and points. At these places, the long swell can start to break at the peak and then peel for a long distance without running out of swell energy. Also, having longer wave lengths, they begin to feel the bottom at a greater depth. This helps the reef, the point, or the canyon form the swell into a perfect peeler.

One spring one of the authors surfed Rincon on a wind swell and became frustrated because the waves would quickly back off, not allowing him to make it down the point. The unusually short rides occurred because the wind

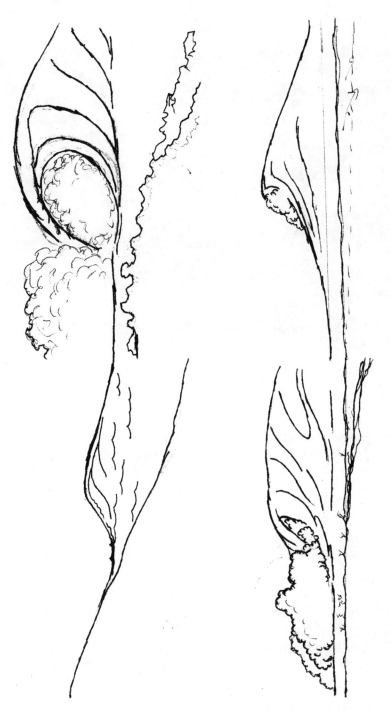

Diagram of waves approaching different bottom contours. The shallower the water, the hollower the wave (relative to wave size).

WindnSea above on a small windswell and below on a clean ground swell. Which looks better?

This three-story wave would like to eat you. Lunada Bay Feb. I, 1986. Photo by Rollo. (Note humanoids on sailboat.)

Pre-shaped beach peaks at warm water jetty in Carlsbad.

Summer windsell peak at Torrance Beach

Swamis on a good ground swell.

Jason Christman tears apart a North San Diego county mush-burger.

Chris Olivas stuffs a tube at Newport.

swells were not long enough to break all the way down the point. But the next day a little ground swell came up from the west, and he got rides which were so long that he had to pull out early from exhaustion.

## The Fundamental Concepts of Good Surf and Its Most Basic Components

The definition of a good surfing wave is one that breaks, not all at once, but peels in a rideable shape for some distance before either closing out or backing off into deep water. Good waves are formed in three ways; by the wind forming the wind swell peaks, by peaks formed when two swells cross from different directions, and by ground swells hitting reefs and points.

Wind swells are short and choppy, and their good shape is pre-made in the swells themselves. They break with good shape upon coming into most beach situations. But, as earlier stated, they usually don't have real good shape when breaking on reefs or at points.

Good shaped surf is also formed when two swells from different directions come in at the same time. Usually there is a ground swell from one direction and a wind swell from the other. When these doubled up swells come into a beach, they form big peaks which peel from the direction of the bigger swells. For example, south swells often appear to be big walls when seen far outside the break, but upon coming closer to the shore, they divide up into many different peaks. They are divided when the smaller swells out of the north or west merge with them and begin to feel the bottom and become steeper.

Note: Many people attribute the peaking of some ground swells to the bottom formations outside the break. This may be true in some situations, but there are three reason why this usually isn't the case. First, sometimes ground swells don't peak up in the noted way on some days, but the next day they do. The bottom changes necessary to cause this change in the breaking pattern in waves probably wouldn't happen except under the most unusual conditions. Second, when you watch beach peaks form and break, it often seems that many of the insiders are coming from a different direction than the sets. Third, during south swells which are "jumping" into peaks, you can often see places which are totally blocked from the south swells, and yet you always find little swells coming in which are out of the north or the west.

Good waves are likewise formed by varied bottom formations and points. A swell will break over an area where the water is shallower before it will break over an area with deeper water. Piles of rocks on the bottom

Well versed in all types of waves, Mark Sharp stuffs the tube of a hollow wave above and while he pushes the top of a mushy wave below.

Seaside Reef in Cardiff.

Salt Creek, "Day of the decade." Photo Marty Victor.

or some other bottom formation which makes an area shallower has the potential to make a good wave because the swell will not all break at once. The wave will break where it is shallow and then will shoulder over the transition area on the edge of the high spot.

Points cause good waves by sticking out from the shore and being at an angle to the incoming swells. Needless to say, the waves begin breaking out at the end of the point where the water is shallow and will continue breaking down the point as the swell continues to encounter shallow water.

## Wind

There are few groups of people who are as in tune with the changing wind conditions as surfers. The wind is the final factor for the creation of good surf. The swell could be out of the proper direction, the tide could be right, the crowd could be small... but the wind must also be right for the surf to be great. Offshores, the best winds for surfing, cause the wave to get steeper and hollower, and they give the ocean a nice, smooth texture. No wind at all is usually the second favorite wind condition. The waves can still be steep and have tubes, though not as noticeable as with offshore winds, and the water will have no texture at all (at least until you wipe out). On some days, when the water is super still and clear, you get the sensation that you are flying while surfing. One of the author's friends searches the coast for this type of condition because when he is speeding along on a long peeler, he likes to fantasize that he is a pelican riding the updraft above a swell.

Sidewinds are generally considered to be O.K. When they are strong, they create little wind-waves which run perpendicular to the breaker. They are miserable to surf because when you are taking off, your rail almost always gets caught in the chop, causing you to eat it. The one plus of sidewinds is that they blow straight into the tube from one direction causing the tube to open wider. If you can make the takeoff, you can often win inside a gaping barrel.

Once one of the authors was night surfing head-high Malibu when the winds were blowing straight into the tubes. Needless to say, it was very cold out there. Also, that night there was an amazing amount of phosphorescence in the water. This is the result of tiny plankton in the water which light up or glow when they are disturbed. Whenever a wave began to break, all of the plankton in the wave would feel the movement of the water and light up. This made the whole wave glow a bright lime green. It was difficult for me to catch the waves, and it was especially hard to make the cold, midnight, side wind takeoffs. And once I was up and standing, I could barely move down the wave because the wind was holding me back.

Mike deNicola makes the best of windy slop.

But soon after the takeoff, the tube would catch up to me and I'd become engulfed. Once in the tube I would begin to accelerate because I was protected from the wind resistance. Essentially, the wind would push me into the tubes and then it would never let me out. Because of the light of the phosphorescence, the womb of the tube was bright green and as light as day. While riding in the tubes, I felt like I was in little spinning rooms which had a black hole in the wall (which led to the shoulder). I clearly remember watching my friend Walt cruising in a tube. I could see every line and detail of his face, but he could not see me as I scratched over the shoulder.

Stiff onshore winds are generally considered to be the worst. They give the wave a lousy, bumpy texture that causes them to break before they get steep, and worst of all, they blow salt water spray into your face the whole time you are paddling out.

## Topography: How to Escape Bad Winds

Like the swell direction, the wind directions can be used to help you find good surf. Over the open ocean the wind blows in a fairly consistent direction, but when in contact with land, it can be considerably altered. Often the surfer needs to find a place where the wind is agreeable in the face of an overall bad wind condition.

Bays are the best places to hide from the wind. When it is blowing sideshore, you can often find good surf at a point or a bay because the wind is blocked or altered. The Hook in Santa Cruz is an outstanding example of a place which is sheltered from the common north wind. It faces perfectly south so that north winds can do nothing but blow straight offshore.

Piers can sometimes block the wind. For example, the Redondo Pier has become famous because it only has good surf when the wind is raging onshore with a big wind swell. The pier is shaped like a horseshoe with a 100 yard stretch of enclosed beach. The wind swells come under the pier and into the beach in their characteristic wind swell peaks, but the wind is effectively blocked by the pier. The one negative aspect of this particular setup is that the pier effectively cages in the hefty crowd which shows up when the waves are good.

Another way to escape bad wind conditions is to find a spot with a lot of kelp growing just outside the lineup. A thick kelp canopy, along with the effect of the kelp's oils on the water, eliminates the troublesome wind bumps and creates glassy conditions. Those of us who live on the West Coast are very fortunate because we have the world's best kelp forests. The one problem you have with hiding from the wind in kelp beds is that kelp is

Dan Wozniak slides into a glassy right. Note the sailboat under full sail and the kelp outside. Kelp is effective at cutting down wind chop.

Guy Trotter surfing the south side of the Oceanside Pier on a north wind. You can sometimes find shelter behind piers. Photo Matt LaZich.

tough to surf through. While on a wave, you can plow into a ball of kelp at any time. This causes the board to stop dead or at least slow down considerably, and the rider continues on at his original speed (until he hits the water).

## Jetties and Harbors

Jetties and harbors are likely to have good surf because they break up the even, sandy bottom. With the changing tides and currents the shallow-water sand moves up and down the beach. The man-made rock formations break up this flow of sand, and this causes it to pile up in some areas to form high spots.

Jetties and harbors can also form good surf by making side waves. This happens when a swell comes in at an angle to the rocks and is deflected. The part of the swell which is bounced off the rocks forms a new swell which meets the unchanged swells. Where the two waves meet, a peak is formed which will peel away from the jetty.

Jetties and harbors are also great because they reduce the down-beach currents. At most beaches, when the swell is up and is coming in at an angle to the beach, a strong current is running parallel to the shore. Jetties break up the water movement so that you aren't quickly swept down the beach. When surfing Huntington Beach during a big south, you often end up a mile or so north of where you paddled out. This is because there are no land formations to break up or slow the shallow water currents. Furthermore, jetties and harbors can act like walls in that they sometimes block the wind and the chop (previously discussed). Generally, these man-made monstrosities are excellent spots to find good surf and to hide from some unfavorable element or condition of the day. Each jetty seems to break differently from the rest, and it is always a good idea to become familiar with the conditions under which each of the local jetties works best.

## Sandbars

Sandbars are probably the most interesting of all surf breaks. They are formed by moving water, and they are so spontaneous that they can come and go in a matter of hours. Most sandbars are made when the waves are coming straight into the beach, i.e., when a west swell hits a west facing beach. Since water comes in perpendicularly to the shore, side currents don't form, and the water is forced to create rivers which flow straight out from the shore.

56th street, Newport Beach. One of the finest jetty set-ups known to mankind. Unknown guy shows how its done. Aug., 1985.

Another unknown guy shows his way of how its done. How did he get there? Photos Dan Wozniak.

Mark Sharp aims...

fires...

and kills at an Oceanside beach break. Photo Matt LaZich.

Oceanside North Jetty on a clean west swell. Photo Matt LaZich.

Oceanside North Jetty circa 1972. Upon his return from Viet Nam, Harry Christman samples a new light-weight shortboard for the first time. Note his incredibly stylish bottom turn. Furthermore, note the kid on the left's beaver-tail, and the grommet's mop on the inside.

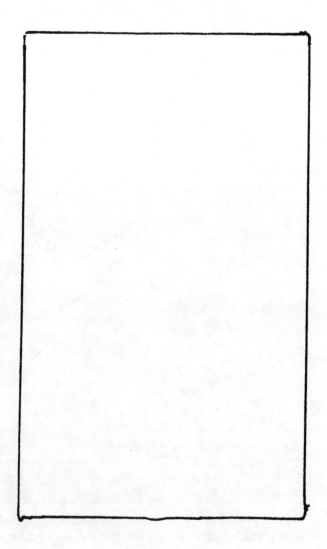

Another good day ruined by blinding fog.

Getting a specific sandbar-producing beach wired takes a lot of time, patience and thought. Sandbars are finicky things, popping up from nowhere at the most unusual times, and even the most consistent ones seem to change from year to year. In the late 70s, when the authors were Torrance beach locals, the best little sand bars would form during Christmas vacation and stay around for about 3 months. But as the years passed, the sand bars became larger and would hold bigger surf, yet were not as well defined or clearly placed along the beach. Also, they often didn't appear until February. Now, or as of last winter (87-88), the bars didn't come at all (and the locals were sad).

Sandbars can be made from rivers which flow into the ocean and by dredges. Often rivers which flow into the ocean carry large amounts of sand which ends up just off the beach. Under the right conditions this sand can create a sandbar which forms point-like waves. Dredges, which are becoming more prevalent along our coast, can be like rivers in the way that they deposit large piles of sand just off the beach. (Note, dredges suck the sand from the bottom by a large pump and dump it somewhere else, usually on the beach so there is more sand for beachcombers.)

## Fog, the Good Time Dampener

Fog is one of those frequent natural elements that surfers have to endure. Fog can really make good swells bad or bad surf even worse. Light onshore winds usually accompany fog, thus making the surf bumpy and sort of blown out. Occasionally in very dense fog, the ocean will be glassy, but then it is difficult to surf because you can't see the waves coming. In the late spring and early summer, fog and low clouds frequently form along the coast. This is generally known as the marine layer. It is caused by the mixing of cold spring ocean water with warm air. Many young surfers look longingly towards the last day of school, eager to lie on the beach, but they are disappointed to find the cold, opaque marine layer blocking the sun. Meanwhile, a short distance inland the fog ends and it is hot and sunny. As the summer progresses, the fog becomes lighter and usually burns off by lunch time. The authors feel that fog is most definitely a drag, but surfing experiences have led them to believe that when the summer surf really turns on, the sun comes out, the chicks appear, cops are friendly, parties happen, the deficit is reduced, and the fog has finished its news for the summer.

Sometimes, when you really want to sun yourself on the beach, you can escape the marine layer. The essential thing to remember about fog is that it does not stretch very far inland nor does it roll over hills. Thus, you must find a beach which is blocked by some sort of land mass. For example, the town of Avalon on the front (east) side of Catalina is almost never bogged in by the marine layer. The marine layer usually comes in with the trade winds, which are out of the northwest, whereas Avalon faces southeast. Cabrillo Beach in San Pedro is likewise often free of fog because it is southeast of the Palos Verdes Peninsula.

# Part II: The Prediction of Surf From Storms Over the Pacific

Almost all waves are created by wind blowing over the ocean. The size of the wave is a factor of the velocity of the wind and the distance which the winds blow over the ocean. The harder the wind or the further the wind blows over the ocean, the bigger the swells will be. But waves are only built when the wind blows faster than and in the same direction as the swells are traveling. There are other other ways in which ocean waves are created, i.e. tide movements and earthquakes, but these types of waves are not really good for surfing and are generally overlooked in this book. (Note, the movement of the tides can sometimes have an effect on the quality of the surf. For example, during a ground swell, there are almost always twenty or so minutes of the most consistent surf of the day when the tide bottoms out. Also, the swell has a tendency to get a little larger during the full moon.)

There are four distinct weather systems which produce surf for us Californians: the large storms of the north and the west, the storms off of the coast of Mexico, the wind swells which roar down from Northern California, and the distant southern hemisphere New Zealand storms.

## Tools of Swell Prediction

Many pieces of information are available to aid you in your attempt to predict surf. But exact swell calling or prediction is very difficult because getting all the needed information to make a precise prediction is nearly impossible. For example, in order to specify exactly how big the waves are going to be from an individual storm, you would have to know how hard the wind is blowing in the middle of the storm and the distance and direction the strong winds traveled. Needless to say, this information is rather difficult to come by. But even if you did have all of the necessary measurements for swell prediction, you would still need an advanced degree in physics to be able to put all of the variables into the proper equations to make sense of it. Frankly, most of us don't have the needed information and mental capacities for precise swell predictions. But we do have outer water buoy readings of the swell and wind, barometer readings, and information from ships that are in the outer waters (though they are actively avoiding storms), measurements and observations from airplanes, and most importantly satellite photos. We receive this information from the weather pages, the radio weather channels, the evening news, and our own observations of the ocean and barometers. Even though the weather information to which we have access is not always perfect or even correct, it is usually quite enough to give us a general idea as to what is going on in the Pacific Ocean.

The goal is to get here. Daybreak at Trestles on the first morning of a swell with two people out. Where were you?

What type of surf is brewing in the Pacific? A small storm in the north may make some surf, but it is out of our swell window. But, the batch of clouds off Baja may deal us a south.

Kit Cossart on a classic winter day at secret spot XQ-36.4.

## Storms

Storms are characterized in weather language as low pressure systems. They have unstable moving air and winds which blow counterclockwise around their center. This is contrasted with high pressure systems, which are warm, less turbulent, and have winds which blow clockwise around the weather system's center. The most important thing to remember is that lows make surf while highs don't. Much has been written about storms, though little is known about them. As Southern Californians we desire high pressure systems to locate themselves over us because the air becomes warm and dry and the wind blows offshore most of the time. As surfers, we like lows to locate themselves off the coast so they can whip up some surf for us. But we do not like lows to make it to the mainland because they give us rain and plenty of onshore winds.

## Barometers

The barometer is helpful because it can indicate how the weather and the wind will be during the day. For example, if you are packing up to go surfing before dawn and want to get a general idea of the day's weather, you can look at the barometer. If there is a high pressure or if the pressure has increased, you can be fairly sure that you will be hanging out on the beach for a few hours because it probably will be nice. But if it reads a low number or if the pressure has dropped, then you may anticipate that a storm is near, and you may even be blown out of the water by the wind. One peculiarity of barometers in southern California is that the barometer needle does not move very much. In the fall of 1988 I moved to Mission Beach, and one of the first things I did to my new pad was hang my barometer on the wall in the living room. After watching the needle do approximately nothing for weeks, my roommates were convinced that it didn't work. I had to defend my little device over and over by arguing that the needle doesn't have to change much to signify a major change in the weather. Sure enough, as they began to look at it the way a weather man would, they were enlightened to the benefits of the barometer. As it turns out, a change of one-tenth of one degree can signify that either a high or a low is moving in.

## The Radio Weather Channel

The monotone voice broadcasters of the radio weather channel can become your best friends. They give the most accurate and up-to-date information available to most surfers. They tell you the positioning of the lows and highs, the size and the direction of the swells and the seas, and the velocities of the winds. (Note, the measurement of the seas refers to the short intervals of the wind chop while the swell measurement gives the information about the bigger intervals between the ground swells.) One of the author's friends has a trick that he once shared with us. He said that one of California's premier long point breaks gets absolutely perfect when the swells are of unusually long intervals. Thus, he listens to the weather channel religiously and immediately runs for it when the intervals get over 17 seconds. Actually, this is not that big of a secret because most points and reefs break best when there is a long interval. When listening, one must have a mental image of the coast to envision how the information relates to the Southern California surf. If you hear that there is a northwest swell of 6 feet, you must realize that they literally mean that the swell is out of the northwest, and only the most northerly facing beaches will have big surf. (Note, recall that what surfers call north is more west than the weather people's north.)

## The Weather Page and Satellite Photo

The most important part of the weather page is the satellite photo. It gives us a clear view of what is happening in our quadrant of the Pacific. We can see the storms forming and moving, and we can determine whether they make it into the swell window. Ideally, we want to see big storms moving straight towards our favorite areas. Sometimes the weather page has a diagram which points out the highs and lows with circles and lines. These are very helpful because they more accurately identify the apexes of the lows and highs. Also, the weather page occasionally notes the pressures of the lows and the highs. These correlate with the strength of the weather system.

The weather page usually includes the surf size of the day as well as the forecast for the next day. If one regularly checks out the surf and reads what the paper says the surf was like, one will quickly come to the conclusion that on some days the weather people measure the backs of the waves, on other days the fronts. A few days a month they measure only the smallest or the largest of the waves, and just every so often they decide to give the measurements of the surf that hit Guam. Furthermore, the surf forecasts are not much better. The authors guess that surfers are not in the weather business. (In all reality, the paper's surf information is not that bad. It is just fun to be critical.) Generally, the reported surf size of the day and the forecast is of little use to the serious surfer because he is usually more in tune with the surf than the forecasters.

## Aggravations or Problems in Storm Watching and Surf Prediction; a Preface to Swell Predicting

Unquestionably the most aggravating facet of storm watching is that good storms are not always out there. Sometimes you can go for months without finding one on the weather page. And, of course, when you are

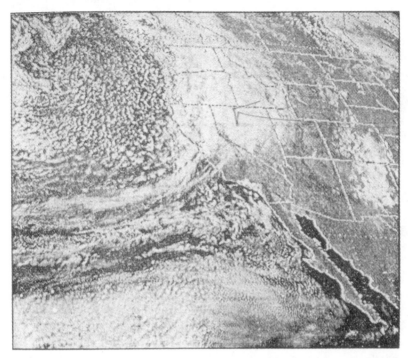

May 29, 1988 The main part of the front went inland north, leaving us nothing.

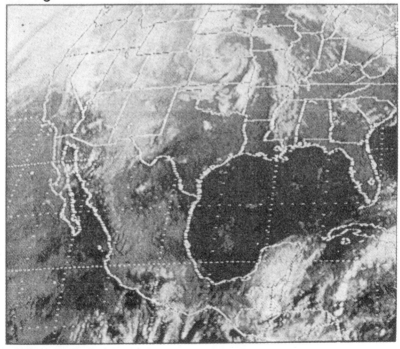

It looks like good tanning in Brownsville and excellent fishing in Missouri.

desperately trying to find a good storm, the surf has been flat for a long time and the non-storm pattern will probably continue. From 1984 to 1986 there was very little surf in Southern California, and looking at a dismal weather page every night for that period just made the situation all the more painful. (Note, the authors actually began this book in the summer of 1985, but gave up for 2 years because of the gross lack of field study - "field study" being good surf.) Fortunately, 1987 - 1988 has been bountiful with lots of surf and storms, but there have been very few really big rideable days.

The second most frustrating feature about storm watching is seeing a surf-producing storm roar away without giving us surf because it is not in our swell window. This occurs very often with wind swells out of the north and deep south swells.

The third most depressing thing about storm watching is the quality of the paper's satellite photo. Often the satellite photo is taken somewhere over Cuba or back East. This doesn't help us understand the surf situation, especially when we are looking for north Pacific storms. Another problem with the satellite photo is that the sensitivities seem to vary. Sometimes the whole ocean appears to be covered with clouds and you can't see what's going on (because the photo is too sensitive), while at other times storms don't appear to look as big as they are (photo not sensitive enough). Also, most satellites do not pick up the low level marine layer (fog) which is prevalent on the coast. So what looks like a nice sunny day may not be. Needless to say, this is nothing but trouble for the surfologist.

Positively the most all around gut-wrenching part of storm watching is waiting for the surf to hit. You can track a storm and be sure the surf is on its way, but you have to wait a few days for it to hit. Wind swells are not that bad, for they hit about 15 hours after they tear up San Francisco, or they arrive the day after the satellite shows the storm coming across Northern California. Northern ground swells, which are produced from a storm much further away, are a little more difficult to handle because the wait is from 4 to 5 days. But some souths are pure hell with waits up to 8 days.

In spite of all of the hardships associated with surf prediction, it always ends up to be a worthwhile chore because there is NOTHING BETTER than precisely predicting a swell and catching it BEFORE ANY ONE ELSE.

## The Instant Surf Wind Swell

Good old wind swells are great because they are simple to predict, you don't have to wait long for surf, and their storms are easy to see and follow. They are most common in the winter months, October - March, but they can

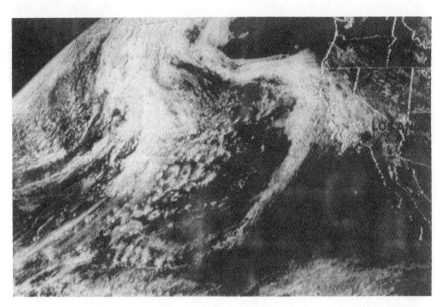

April 30, 1989, above, a clear wind swell storm is coming towards us and we probably will get some head-high peaks in about eighteen hours.    March 30, 1989, below, a spiraling front progresses inland but keeps to the north yielding smaller waves for us.

Jim Hart cuts loose on a fun summer wind swell at Torrance Beach, summer of 1984.

Prior knowledge will eventually payoff.

come in at any time. Wind swell storms are seen as bands of clouds which originate off Oregon and march down the coast. A diagrammed weather map will show it as a front which stretches from the coast out into the ocean. One can observe these storms as they move down the coast by listening to the weather channel or by watching the weather news or the satellite photos. Usually the surf will hit the day after the storm is pictured in Northern California, or 15 hours after it hits San Francisco.

One important factor in studying the wind swell storm is its placement off the coast. The storm must stretch out past Point Conception so that the waves can make it into our swell window. Many storms are too close to the Northern Coast to give anything except bad weather. One thing which is characteristic of many wind swells is the wind behind the initial front. Sometimes the wind will blow for days after the front has passed. These winds can be expected if there are blotchy clouds (which just look like wind) behind the front in the satellite photo. Regular wind swells seldom last for more than 15 hours, and often you will paddle out at dawn when the swell is up and come in a few hours later with surf only one-half the early-morning size.

## North and West Swells

North and west swell storms are distinguished from wind swell storms because they rage further out to sea and are much bigger. And because they are further out to sea, their swells are cleaner, more lined up, and have longer intervals. Usually these storms or lows appear to just sit out there for days. This makes their surf difficult to predict because there are no clouds to mark the progress of the swells as they roll towards land. But when these storms do move, we want them to come straight towards us. The biggest surf is pushed in the direction in which the storm is heading.

There is a knack to predicting what day the surf will hit. Usually it takes around 5 - 7 days from the first sighting of the storm to the time it breaks on the beach. With practice, you get a sort of unconscious understanding of predicting the surf's time of arrival.

Most north and west swells make it into Southern California's swell window, but they are almost always considerably bigger north of Point Conception. They gradually get larger the farther you travel north. There is one thing, however, which can totally flatten out any surf which was made by a low. This is a high pressure between us and the storm. Several times the author's early predictions were inaccurate; they called for a swell and made big plans for nothing because the surf was blocked by a high. The wind from highs blow in the opposite direction as the winds from a low, and the high's winds flatten out what the low's winds created.

The goal: a big perfect day with you and your friend sharing a break just as a swell is hitting. Pictured are Tom Wegener and Steve May (sitting) at their favorite big wave break.

Incognito shot of Bill Burke at 12-15 ft. Ocean Beach near San Francisco. (12-15 ft. backs!)  Quote: "I think I'll wait a while."  Photo Mark Ward.

This is a big storm. Truly immense. Simply monstrous. Gargantuan. Time to take out a life insurance policy. This storm produced the biggest waves of the decade. The low extends from the Aleutians to the same latitude as Hawaii.

Epic winter of 1982-83. Febuary, 1983, LA County. Will it ever happen again? Can you see the guy on the second wave? Photo Neil Gegna.

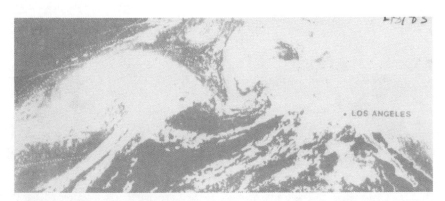

Feb. 8, 1983. The great storm . . . huge and it will make huge surf. This swell ripped up the whole coast.

Feb. 17, 1983. Febuary '83 had so much weather that it baffled scientists and meteorologists, while keeping surfers out of school, work, doctors' offices, and court appearances.

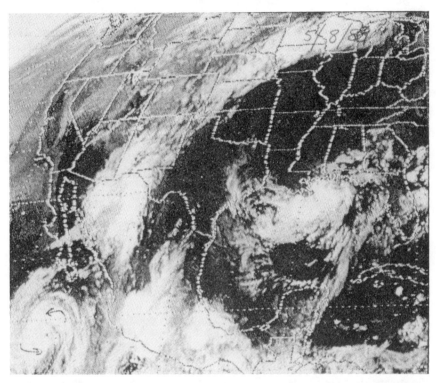

Mexican chubassco raging off the tip of Baja. Unfortunately, we Southern Californians never got waves from this storm because it didn't make it into our swell window. Notice how the swirls go in a counter clockwise manner.

# The Long and Clean South Swell

Some people's favorite aspect of summer is warm weather. Students look forward to summer for vacation. Perverts await forward to summer in order to ogle at those skinny, voluptuous creatures in string bikinis. The surfer's favorite feature of the summer is the south swell. South swells are almost always clean, lined up, and perfectly surfable. Furthermore, Southern California is extremely open to them.

Souths are produced by hurricanes and storms off Mexico. The most prevalent swells are formed from storms which begin off Puerta Vallarta and move northwest until they are around 500 miles west of Cabo San Lucas. Then they either move west towards Hawaii or northwest toward us. Either way, they eventually dissipate into cold water as they move away from Cabo San Lucas. As Southern Californians, we hope the storms move far enough west to get into our swell window, but we also want them to move in a somewhat northward direction so that we get the waves they produce.

These hurricanes are easy to follow on the map and generally last a relatively long time. Also, the media has a tendency to make a big deal of these storms. The major problem is that they may rage for days before they make it to our swell window. Thus, many storm watchers get high blood pressure anticipating their arrival to the necessary position.

Many southern storms do not make it to our window. The summer of 1986 proved that. Thus, we do not primarily watch the size or consistency of the storms but their placement and direction. Generally, as the summer progresses, more of the storms will make it into our swell window and march northward.

Once a storm has made it into the window, the waiting game begins. How long will it be before the swells make it to our coast? You may think that you could estimate the time of arrival by multiplying the swell speed by the distance they will travel. This is not really true because swells have one rather odd behavior: one wave, as it is rolling along, will often disappear or melt into the wave behind it. This phenomenon throws the distance times velocity theory out. The authors have discovered, from purely empirical studies, that it usually takes 5 days for the storms off Cabo San Lucas to hit us, and 8 days for storms further south. Getting this amount of time is not as easy as one may think, and it occasionally may appear to be wrong. Storms sometimes run one right after another. We may be getting south swells while there is a storm raging, thus giving the impression that the present swells are coming from the storm at hand.

Bill Burke surfing and Jim Heubner on a clean south swell that made it into Santa Barbara's swell window.

Chris Olivas pulls some summer air in Imperial Beach.

Sandra raised the hopes of surfers back in September of 1985. She is producing some epic surf for much of Baja, and if she comes towards Southern California, we will get some big surf too.

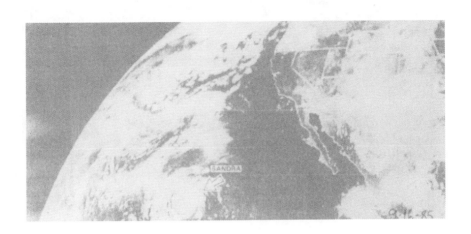

Oh well, another dud.  Sandra moves off to Hawaii leaving us with smaller surf.  But now Terry comes on the scene on September 17.

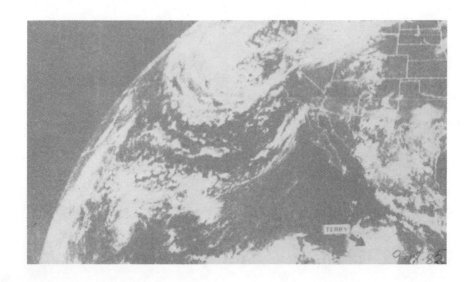

Terry spins madly off mainland Mexico and increases in strength as it moves towards Baja.

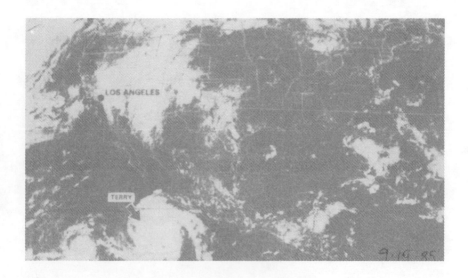

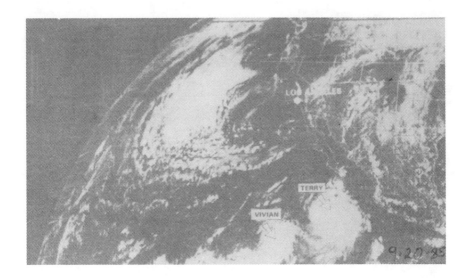

Terry spawns Vivian.  Not a good place to sail into.

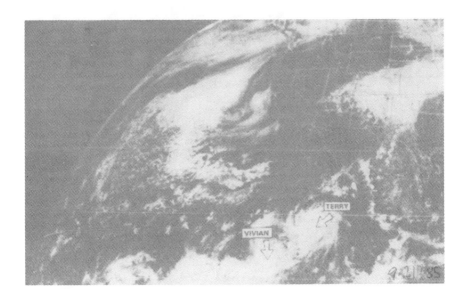

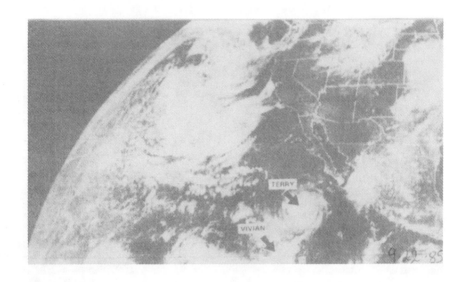

Terry continues to linger off Cabo San Lucas.  Will it ever move into our window?

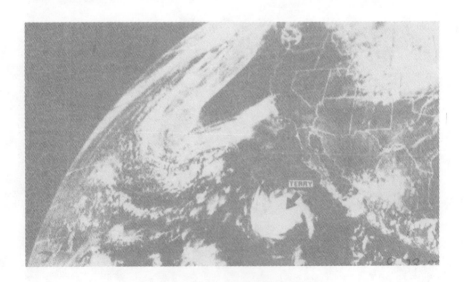

Yes, it appears that Terry will give us surf. By the 25th it has
definitely moved into our window.

Here is an oddity. Octave stayed so close to Baja that it was out of San Diego's swell window. But all the south facing beaches north of San Onofre were excellent.

On July 22, 1988, Daniel made it into our window.

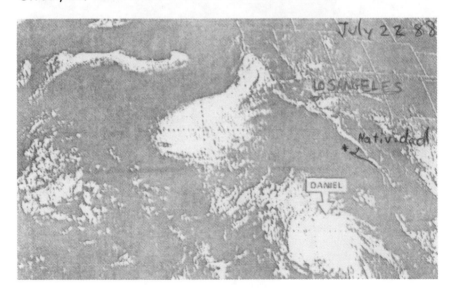

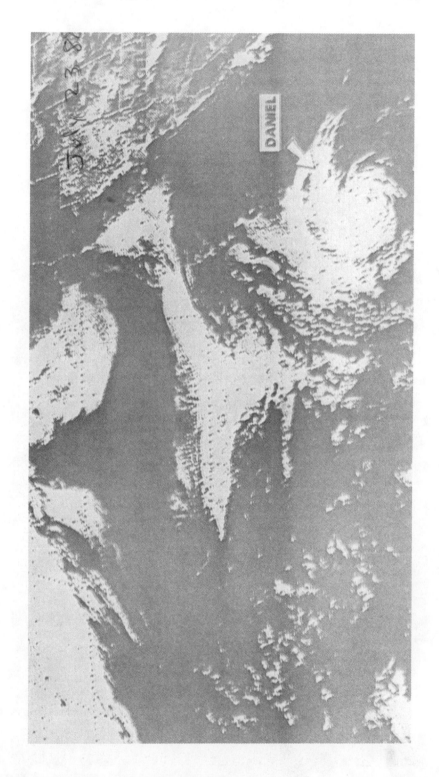

Hurricane Daniel, one of the few wave producers inthe summer of 1988. Eric Stoops caught the tail end of this swell on the Isle de Natividad.

Not all south swells are caused by the classic summer hurricane. Sometimes they come from regular storms off Mexico, which can occur seemingly any time of the year. The cloud formation of these storms looks like a blotchy group of innocent clouds, but really quite a storm is brewing. These storms don't move much and often are in the swell window.

## The New Zealand Swell

The other source of a good south swell lies in the southern hemisphere, where swells are produced by intense low pressure storm systems off the Antarctic. Our summer is actually winter for our friends south of the equator. The first thing to know about New Zealand swells is that they are very hard to predict. Actually, this is not quite true. Almost everybody is constantly "predicting" that one will "hit any day," and they have no problem "predicting" them. However, there is generally no substance to their words and, unfortunately, they are almost always wrong. It is extremely difficult to plot a New Zealand storm and make a valid surf prediction.

Most newspapers do not carry global satellite photos. And even if you find the necessary photos, it is difficult to predict the surf due to the weather between you and the storm. For example, the waves may be knocked down by northeastern winds long before they get near us. The other problem with "southern hemys" is that they are relatively rare in occurrence.

Despite the complex natural ingredients required for a New Zealand swell, these swells are often the most lined-up and well-formed swells we get. They travel across the world, pulverizing Tahiti, Hawaii, Mexico, California, etc. For instance, in June of 1988, author Bill Burke and girlfriend's family took a trip to Tahiti and the Society Islands. We had chartered a sailboat to cruise the islands. At one time we planned to cross the channel from Raetea to Bora Bora but were not able to for two days because the one and only harbor entrance was closed out by some unusually big southern hemisphere surf (about quadruple overhead). I grew anxious because I knew the surf was good somewhere. Upon my return to California, I spoke with friends who had surfed the same swell at about double overhead for a couple of days. It was a drastic reduction in size, but one of the few south swells to hit that whole summer.

In summary, there is one rule which we have found to be true: That is that you should never believe the gossip about New Zealand swells. Instead, just be happy when they unexpectedly hit.

The authors exhibit how to make the best of poor surf. Above is Bill Burke on the nose, and below is Tom Wegener about to be zip-locked at Oceanside pier. The swell was 2-3 ft. out of the south and hideously inconsistent. Photos Neil Gegna.

Author Bill Burke and photographer Neil Gegna headed north the next day. Same swell 200 miles north at Malibu. Weak south swells can be frustrating. Pictured is Leo Carillo. When we pulled up, a solid six wave over head set rifled through the rock and deceived me into stopping and surfing - and getting a $28 parking ticket. There wasn't another set over shoulder high for over an hour.

June 15, 1988. It took 6-7 days for the surf to get to us, but when it did, it was a perfect five to ten feet high and it lasted for three days. Notice how far south of Cabo the storm is.

This book is about how to avoid this: shoulder-hopping geeks at Malibu.

# El Nino

The El Nino of 1982-83 brought California the most rain and the biggest surf in years. It also introduced catastrophic drought to Australia and Africa, and torrential flooding to North and South America. What caused this global weather disturbance? An annual current flowing past Ecuador called "El Nino," which in English means "the child." South Americans often experience this warm current around Christmas (birth of the Christ child), hence the name.

In 1982-83 the current began early and ended late, thus causing widespread weather change. El Nino is basically a climatic event which occurs when normal westerly trade wind patterns break down along the equator and reverse their direction, thus causing the equatorial surface current to shift as well.

In the spring of 1982 this phenomenon occurred in a powerful manner. Normal westerly trade patterns broke down as did predominant high pressure areas. They were replaced by easterly trades and a low pressure system that settled in the central Pacific. This reverse in the trades is known as southern oscillation. Through a technical process called the "Kelvin Wave," huge amounts of warm water spread along the equator for 8,000 miles. This warm water is pushed further north by the reversed trade winds, and the sea level is raised as much as eight inches as far north as Canada.

The warm water brought a variety of subtropical marine species to northern waters. Barracuda patrolled Oregon waters, red crabs washed ashore from Baja Norte to Ventura, yellowfin and bigeye tuna were caught in the San Pedro channel, and the northwestern salmon fishery was destroyed. El Nino also carried drought to Australia and Africa, causing whole economies to nearly crumble, and strife and starvation to many families and farmers. Ecuador and coastal South American countries suffered intense floods and mudslides. Drought prevailed in the northeastern United States, and temperatures became bitterly cold.

Storm after storm brought radical surf to Southern California. Spots that seldom get overhead waves were maxed-out with perfect sets. While many Aussies groveled in a dust bowl, Californians dug their way out of mud. Surfers lost jobs and cut school to get to the surf. Looking back at the years between 1983 and 1989, I doubt many regret skipping a dentist appointment, school, or a wedding date, because there has not been a winter like 82/83 since. The years of 1983/86 saw a mild El Nino, and it brought us some epic surf. However, it was not nearly as relentless as the big El Nino of 1982/83. Scientists are still bewildered by the phenomenon because of its illusive nature. Yet they claim that better understanding of El Nino will help to make more accurate long-range forecasts.

# Part III: Short Stories Which Further Animate the Information and Ideas of the Earlier Chapters

Many factors are involved in the creation of an excellent surf session. The surfologist must have vast knowledge of such things as storms, swell windows, land topography, and swell intervals to be able to consistently find good surf. Furthermore, a healthy attitude helps the surfer have the best possible time once he hits the surf. The stories which follow are real life experiences which describe how to predict storms, how to think about finding surf given the elements of the day, and how to have the most fun while surfing.

## South swells at Santa Cruz Island

In the summer of 1988, Jeff Barnett and his friends were happily surfing Mar-Meadows on the west side of Santa Cruz Island. The surf was overhead and clean, and several lobsters awaited them for lunch on the boat. Generally, things were going well. But within a short time the right breaking waves they were surfing began to close out on the sets. "Why is this?" he and his friends wondered. A south must be starting to hit, they reasoned. The weather channel's buoy readings soon confirmed their theory. Since the size of the swells was growing, they quickly powered down to a break called "Yellow Banks" on the southern tip of the island. Pointing southeast, this point doesn't break often, but on a deep south it comes alive. Also, because the point faces south east, the trade winds blow off shore.

Sure enough, they found double overhead sets spinning down the point. Their good situation had just become better. They surfed the three hundred yard long grinders for two days, and only one person joined their mini-crowd during their stay. (The moral of the story is that there is good surf in California for those who have the time and the know-how to find it).

## Government Point: March 1984

How far should you go to get good surf? This question constantly plagues the surf hunter. "Should I go to my local breaks where it is o.k., or should I travel and maybe find perfect surf elsewhere?" The more knowledge you have of surfology the better you will be able to make these decisions.

Tom and I attended Marymount Palos Verdes Junior College from 1983 to 1985. This small educational institution has a beautiful view of Catalina Island and the San Pedro channel, and on clear days you can see all the way from Dana Point in the south to Point Dume to the north. This is an excellent place to view swell direction. One pleasant Friday afternoon in late March of 1984 I walked to class, gazing at the deep blue ocean and wonder-

Jeff Barnet and a friend paddle out to a spot called "Yellow Banks" on Santa Cruz Island.

ing how the surf was doing. I was on my way to a math class in which I was about to face a quiz. Lost in my thoughts, I was suddenly startled by three of my friends driving by screaming, "COJO!" My stomach dropped. I could see that a surf trip was imminent. When Tom Wegener calls it, you have to go, no questions asked. (Note: Cojo Point is a perfect wave break area in the Holister Ranch near Santa Barbara. The Ranch is a 14-mile stretch of private beach with many good breaks. The owners of this land do not like trespassers, and they are especially hostile to surfers.)

After my math quiz I went home and put together my gear in preparation for a long hike. Tom picked me up in his truck, and we collected several more lads for the trip. The six of us went to a raging party by Torrance beach put on by our friend Mark Ward. Mark's parents own a parcel at Hollister Ranch. Many fiascos have been attributed to him by ranch security personnel when good surf was running and his friends came to get the benefit of the waves. "DON'T USE MY NAME WHEN YOU GET CAUGHT," he said. "We won't," we replied.

After the bash with music by the King Pins, we loaded up and headed north. Tom was nominated driver. Two of the lads smoked cigars and played the guitar, while others made a feeble effort at sleeping. It was 3:00 a.m. when we reached Jalama, a state park immediately north of the Ranch. The moon was full and bright, the wind was offshore, and the surf was overhead. We walked down the train tracks into the Ranch with old longboards, cigars, PBJ's, a gallon of water, and the inspirational energy nurtured by thoughts of the adventure ahead.

It took two and one-half hours to reach the Point Conception lighthouse well inside the Ranch. It was eerie. Every half hour or so a train would scream past. Being near the tracks when a train passes is one of the spookiest feelings I know. We looked toward Cojo, another three or four miles down the road. It was getting light. We opted to run for Government Point since it was closer and it was getting late. We walked down the beach and watched as perfect overhead peelers wound down the point. Without any hesitation we suited up and hit the waves. It was clear that we were utterly exhausted as we paddled out. One of our members was too tired and said he'd wait on the beach. The rest of us surfed perfect waves for forty-five minutes. Then a dark green Ranch ranger truck pulled up.

Our friend on the beach was sound asleep on the rocks. The officer didn't wake him up initially but started to collect our belongings and throw them in his truck. "Party's over," one of our friends said. We headed for the beach nervously and stood before the ranger, feeling quite stupid. The man placed us all under arrest and taunted us verbally with the thought that perhaps he could goad us into mouthing off. We apologized for being on his land and told him what nice cows he had. The man became compassionate. But just as his mood was starting to mellow, the friend that had been sleeping awakened and said, "Wait! We know Mark Ward." We all broke into suppressed laughter. The man's eyes looked right through us.

"I should have known," he said. He proceeded to take our pictures and fingerprints to be kept on file for trespassing surfers. "If you are caught a second time, you go to jail. You have two hours to get off this land." He gave us our stuff back and said, "No, you can't have a ride." It took us four hours to make it back to Jalama. Four hours of excruciating torture, for forty-five minutes of perfect surf. A word of advice to our readers: If you try it, you will get caught. And don't tell them you know Mark Ward.

## A Big Morning at Haggerty's

Early one morning I was sleeping peacefully when a friend of mine, Pat Kilroy, began banging on my window. "Tom, Tom, let's go surfing." Still being young and vivacious, I immediately jumped out of bed, gathered my things, and hopped in the car without a second thought, even though there was a good hour and a half before dawn.

We drove the usual route to the beach, but something was different this morning. Looking out over the cliffs from the road above Haggerty's, we could see waves breaking as we drove. This was unusual because I'd never been able to see waves break from that part of the road before. I reasoned that the surf must be big today. My heart began to sink with fear and anticipation. How big is it? It couldn't be extremely big, for it was small last night. Because of the darkness I couldn't quite get a grip on the size of the surf, even after we had pulled up to Haggerty's and looked at it for a while. I guessed that it was about one and one-half times over head. Thinking that it was not too treacherous, I decided to suit up and paddle out in the dark. From the shore break things didn't look threatening. Safely making it to the take-off area, I thought that I was in for a nice, fun surf session. But as I was feeling comfortable, I watched the whole horizon turn from a deep navy blue to pitch black, and then with a thundering crash everything turned white. Within seconds I was completely beaten.

But I survived my punishment, and seeing that it was just beginning to get light, I decided to paddle back out and try again. But this time I paddled way outside. As it turned out, the sets were almost triple over-head , perfectly shaped, and amazingly ferocious. Once it was light I raised my gumption level and began to take off on the sets. They had steep drops and long, clean spinning shoulders which were just right for a sophomore in high school who wanted to learn about big waves.

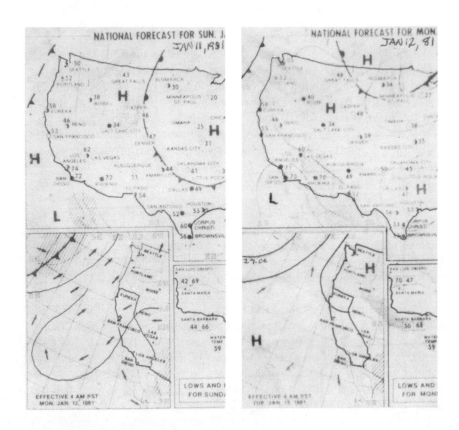

January 11, 1981, eight days before the swell, and already the front is clear on the map. The anticipation of a swell begins. But, there is a considerably large high pressure system sitting off the coast. Fortunately, this high was not strong enough to blow down the swells or hold back the storm.

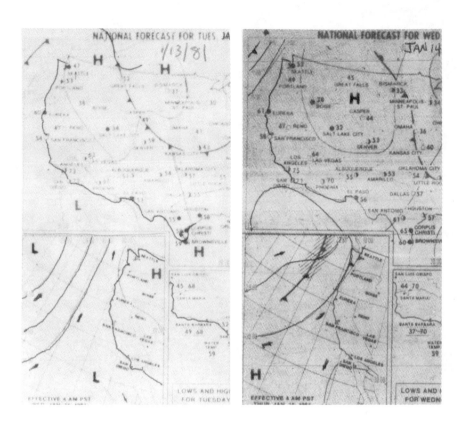

January 15. The storm has been raging for at least four days, and it still has not hit land. This is a good sign because the longer the storm stays out to sea, the bigger the surf.

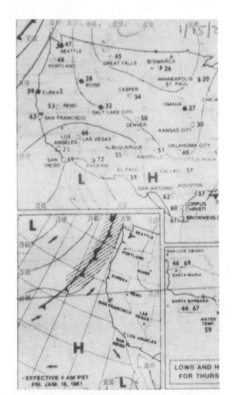

A perfect grinder a Haggerty's.

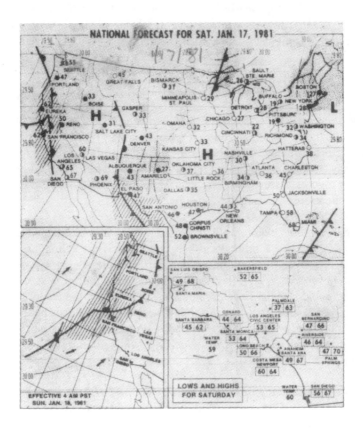

NATIONAL FORECAST FOR SAT. JAN. 17, 1981

EFFECTIVE 4 AM PST
SUN. JAN. 18, 1981

LOWS AND HIGHS
FOR SATURDAY

January 17. Though the storm's strongest part seems to have hit Northern California, we got some surf because the front stretched well into our swell window. Even though Northern California was hit with bad weather from the storm, we remained dry and calm. We got the surf from the storm, but the storm itself did not make it to us because it was blocked by Point Conception.

January 19. The surf came up and very few people were on it. Because the swell was produced so far away and it was so long in the making, the swells we received were long and clean.

We surfed well into first period without the usual relentless crowd and mean locals because we were the only people who knew the swell had hit. If I had been watching the weather maps, this surf would not have been such a surprise. A large low pressure system had been moving in from the north west for a week, and just by looking at the diagrams, I should have noted that a swell was due.

## The Best Birthday Gift

The winter of 1986-1987 was not a good year for big surf, and by March 5th , my birthday, I had figured that I would not surf any waves of the large variety before summer. On the morning of my birthday, I woke to go surfing extra early because my girlfriend and I had made plans to have a big birthday breakfast together. But when I looked at the daybreak swells, the entire out-look for the morning changed.

Long, beautiful, clean swells were thundering in and completely closing out Tamarack and the other local breaks. "This is it," I thought, "finally a swell. Hurry Tom, get out there before something changes. But wait a minute, I have plans." I felt terrible as I woke Kim to inform her of the situation. We could share a later breakfast or a lunch - or she could even come with me. Being the ultimate girlfriend, it was not long before she understood and the problem was resolved (we ended up having a great lunch). (Side theme; don't be afraid to change plans when the surf is good - it is usually well worth the hassle.)

"With the swell being this lined up and clean, where is the spot?" I thought to myself. After seeing the ant trail of surfers running for Swamis, about two to three times over head, I decided to head to Black's.

Black's was simply majestic with absolutely huge peaks and long, peeling lefts. I could even see the swells building from the top of the trail (very un-usual for Black's). The peaks were in the usual area, north of the trail, but the paddle-out zone was a little south of the road. On my second attempt I made it out, and I watched for no more than 30 seconds before a giant per-fect peak came directly to me. Not really ready, I took off, made a long screaming bottom turn, and pulled up high in the pocket with a long wall in front of me. The characteristic Black's lip pitched way out, and the wave let me ride in its belly for at least 100 yards before giving me the characteristic Black's beating. When I finally popped up, I had a big, glowing smile and a warm feeling that the winter had just become complete.

By 9:00 a.m. the onshore winds were blowing about 30 miles per hour and the surf had flattened out. No more big waves were to be found that winter in Southern California, and once again, the rules of the surfologist held true. First, when the surf is big and good, go surfing then - not in an hour, not

march 18,

Taken at 12:30 a.m. PST Saturday National Oceanic and Atmospheric Administration / Associated Press

march 2 87

Taken at 12:30 a.m. PST Sunday National Oceanic and Atmospheric Administration / Associated Press

March 2, 1987. A large storm begins its trek towards us, but this storm is from an unusually low latitude. If the surf makes it to us, it will be out of the west.

103

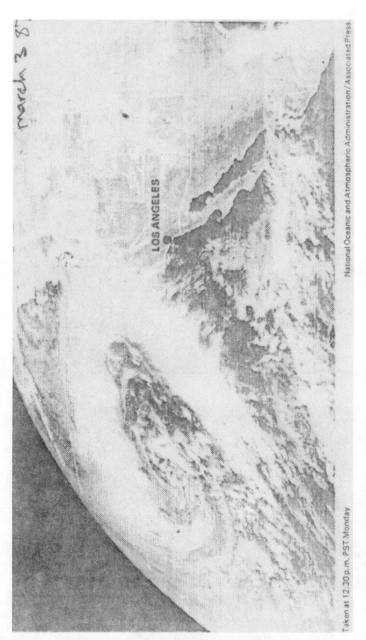

*march 3 8[?]*

LOS ANGELES

National Oceanic and Atmospheric Administration / Associated Press

Taken at 12:30 p.m. PST Monday

March 3. The storm looks like it has gained some energy and it appears that surf is imminent. But, it also looks like the storm itself is going to make it to us. This means we may be in for some bad weather and the surf may be blown out.

March 4.   The storm is a short distance off of our coast and it is in our swell window. Also, and there is no high which could block the surf.

March 5.   The biggest day of 1987: solid 18 foot high peaks at Blacks! Note, this satellite photo appeared in the paper the same day the swell hit. This is possible because the photo was taken on March 4. Satellite photos are taken the day before they appear in the newspaper. This is an important fact to consider when predicting surf. If a surfologist had thought this photo was actually taken on March 5, he would not have run for the surf until the 6th, and missed the swell.

tomorrow, but right at the time you find out that it is perfect. Second, watch the weather page. The satellite photos clearly show that surf was due that morning.

## Big, Perfect Surf

There is one thing for which the authors will never forgive themselves: missing good surf because we did something less important. Most non-surfers say, "Oh, don't worry, the surf will be like this next week" or, "It gets this good all the time." They are wrong. Perfect days where the sun is out, few people are around, the surf is up - are very rare. You are lucky to get more than one or two perfect days a year. The perfect day is something a surfer never forgets, and it is something he may relive every day for the rest of his life. The perfect day does not only have value for the day but for the memory.

When I was in high school, on several days, the surf was perfect, really perfect. And I thought showing up at school was more important than surf-ing. Well, I was wrong. Perfect days were more important than school. For most surfers, surfing is a love or obsession which is one of the top 2 or 3 priorities in their lives, and to fulfill the honor of surfing a perfect day is one of the best things ( if not the best thing) which can happen to a person. One day at high school, I should have known, was not as important to me as one perfect surfing session. I'm not saying that I shouldn't have gone to high school. But I do think that I could have taken a few days off to surf perfect waves and still have done just as as well in school. Life is too short to let per-fect days slip by.

If someone asked me what I was doing in school on any one of the days in May, 1982, I would not remember. I remember many things about school, but not really any particular day. On the other hand, perfect days are dif-ferent. I can remember almost every detail about the perfect days I had, and I can even clearly recall my frustrations when I was in school thinking about the surf I was missing. Don't let the trivial, day-to-day obligations get you into a rut which keeps you from good waves.

## Jalama

One Christmas vacation when we were seniors in high school, Tom, Jay Nicholson, and I found ourselves sitting around Torrance beach complaining about the excessively small surf. We faced a Santa-Ana heat wave, glassy conditions, and a perfectly lined up one foot swell. Even at that time we were surf predictors, and we figured that it would be bigger north of Point Conception because it is more open to north swells. The continental shelf also runs closer to the shore in that region, which means that there is less friction between the ocean floor and the moving swells.

106

February 28, 1989. A storm that was hard to call.

On Tuesday, February 28, things looked promising. There were two lows straight off our coast, and according to the diagrammed weather map, there were no highs to block the surf. Thursday night or Friday morning we should have some big surf. These weather patterns reminded me of the day I surfed Black's almost exactly two years earlier. Was there going to be a repeat performance by the surf?

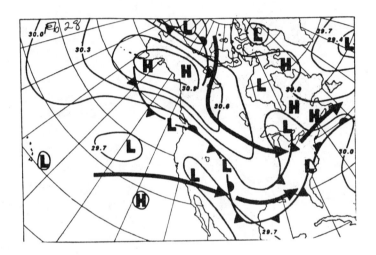

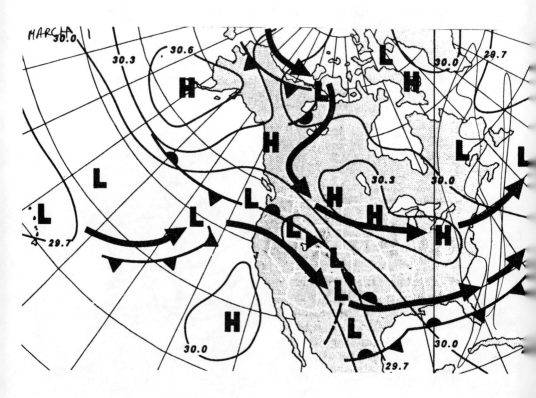

Wednesday, March 1. A high moved over us, but this didn't seem to be a problem because it wasn't strong. The surf should be able to roll through it, we thought. We were expecting big, semi-lined -up groundswells with short intervals from the west.

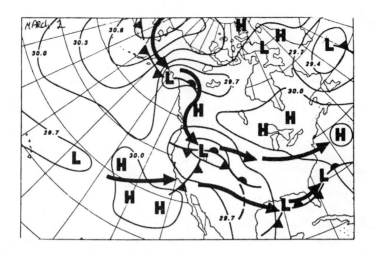

Thursday, March 2. My heart sank as I checked the surf in the morning. The surf had picked up, but so did the onshore winds. The whole storm system had made it to the coast. Point Conception didn't block this storm. By Thursday afternoon it was very gray and stormy with no rideable surf.

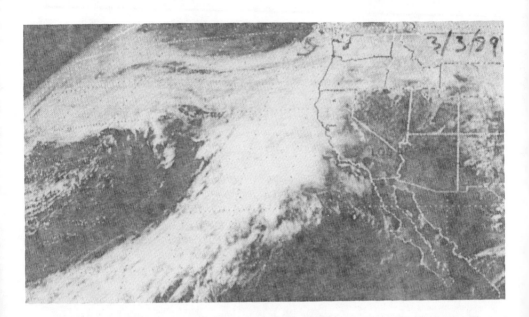

Keep in mind that satelite photos in the newspaper are taken about twenty four hours prior to you seeing them. This photo was taken around the time Tom was checking the surf, and soon eating donuts.

The winter of 1988-89 was not one of California's better years. As a matter of fact, it has been considered the worst winter of the last quarter century. Some fishermen have told me that the lack of good, solid surfing storms this year was caused by an anti-El Nino condition. (Fishermen generally know their weather.) We received an extra strong current of cold water coming from Alaska. Big storms are generated by warm water, as we have seen in the El Nino years. The fishermen also told me that the gray whales traveled all the way down to Cabo San Lucas and Mazatlan this year before they found the water conditions they liked. Usually they only swim half way down Baja to Scamon's Lagoon.

We all needed to get out of town for a while, so we loaded up my old 1963 Ford Galaxy 500 and headed north. To our surprise, the surf had picked up that night as we drove by perfect, head high, moon-lit Rincon. We pressed on to our destination of Jalama, the first beach with public access north of Point Conception. Sure enough, on our arrival that evening the surf was bigger than down south. We checked the surf quickly and went to sleep.

The next morning it was cold. REALLY COLD! The offshore seemed too be flowing from Aspen, Colorado, as it was us chilling to the bone. The surf was better than at Torrance, but it was not good enough to warrent leaving of our cozy sleeping bags. It was just overhead with offshore winds and a mean shore pound.

We sat on the shore and watched the tide begin to drop. As it did, we noticed a small creek flowing into the ocean, and just outside this was a high spot. As the tide dropped further, the waves began to cap (break out further) on the high spot, and a riptide started where the river emptied.

Seeing what was about to happen, we braved the cold and put on our cold, wet, and sandy wetsuits. This groveling process is is perfectly miserable, yet it is not enough to keep the durable surf from good surf. Within the hour all of the elements came together; the wind was offshore and the swell was clean. A deep channel gave the waves perfect shape, and the shallow high spot and the moving rip made the waves especially hollow and powerful. Needless to say, we had one of the greatest sessions of all time, and nobody else paddled out.

Jay got cold and went in to take some super 8 movies of the festivities. Unfortunately, the movies still remain lost in the bowels of the Wegener household.

After about two-and-a-half hours the tide had dropped too much, so the waves began to close out beyond the high spot and the channel. Paradise was lost in a matter of minutes as a torrential riptide formed. We came in for a round of scrambled pancakes, O.J., and a four hour nap.

## December 10, 1988: Oceanside Longboarders' Board Meeting

Every now and then, when the weather gets nice and the surf is fun, the Oceanside Longboard Surfing Club charges the beach and shows the rest of the world how to have a good time. Early in December of 1988, the club noticed that the conditions were right, so without hesitation they called a beach barbeque. A high pressure system had moved over Southern California and there was a small but clean north swell running.

111

Two Oceanside Longboard Club members pull mellow turns on a nice day at Oceanside's North Jetty. Both photos Christman.

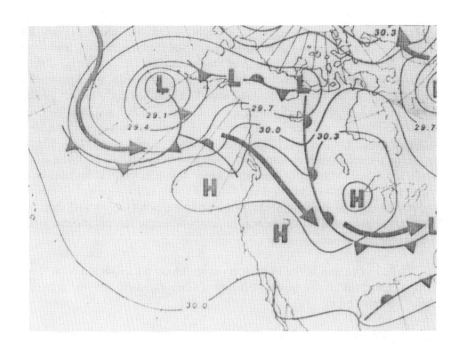

The high pressure over the coast gives us warm sunny skies, but, they also hold back the surf and the storms. Notice far north the low is relative to other storms shown in this book.

These people know how to do it right. On this morning they hit Oceanside's north jetty in the morning and surfed their brains out. The large group effectively took over a section of the beach and filled it with good surfing vibe (meanwhile, many other North County breaks were unusually uncrowded). After surfing, the gang and their families got together on the beach and talked about surfboards, cooked, and ridiculed whoever ever appeared to have gained weight. The whole time everyone was working up a mean appetite. On this day, Donald Takayama, a world famous chef and surfer, made the scene with one hundred pounds of fresh swordfish marinated in Surfer's Choice Marinade (unquestionably the best marinade known to mankind). The club barbequed the fish and fixed other foods of all shapes and sizes to fill the club members, who also come in all shapes and sizes. A mean grind prevailed on the beach, ending with many full bellies and more overweight type comments.

This has to be one of the best events ever. I have a lot to learn from these surfing elders, for after a quarter century of surfing, they've got the concepts pretty well mastered.

## Surfing Etiquette: Who Gets the Most Right to the Wave

When this book was still in the making (scattered all over my room in little pieces), I asked my friends what they thought should be included. To my surprise, they almost always requested that I add a section explaining surfing etiquette. This was especially true of my friends in college who had just moved out here and wanted to learn how to surf.

There are two competing rules for who gets the wave. Some people think that he who catches the wave first gets ownership, while most think that the person who takes off the furthest back gets it. Two policies exist behind the two rules: First, we want possession to go to the surfer who will get the longest and most critical ride. Second, we want a clear and easy rule so there is the least amount of confusion as possible.

The "first one up" rule seems to be a holdover from the longboarding era. One's placement on the wave during the takeoff was not as important for longboarders because they could catch the wave early and fade into the best part of the wave easily. And because they took off so early, it was usually easy to tell who was standing first.

The "furthest person back" rule is most sensible for modern shortboard surfing because wave positioning is very important. Short boards catch the wave later so they can't fade very much, and thus the furthest person back has the best chance of getting into the most critical part of the wave. Also,

Above is the classic maneuver known as the "snake." Below, a longboarder, Harry Christman, pulls a flawless fade. Photo Christman.

with shortboards, it is difficult to see who stands up first because people usually stand up at the same time. But it is always clear as to who is the furthest person back in the peak.

Over all, the modern rule is the better one because it ensures that everyone can get waves. Also, it is the safest because it is very clear as to who has the most right to the wave. For the most part, everyone follows this rule. (And the first one up is usually the furthest one back anyway.)

Sometimes it is not clear as to who can take off on the wave in spite of the rule. For example, the guy who is the furthest back may not be able to make it to where you want to take off. If he couldn't make it, you have the right to go for it, but if he can make it, you must pull back. Unfortunately, it is not clear if the guy will be able to make it to you. In situations like this, use your best judgment, and remember, better safe than sorry.

One of my friends, Jeff Barnett, was once surfing a good-sized day at Trestles when he got into a skuffle with another guy. Jeff had dropped into a juicy wave, and after he had planted his edge in a solid bottom turn, he began to drive up the wave to do an off-the-lip. Just then he noticed a guy still trying to paddle into his wave - and directly in Jeff's path. At this point Jeff was committed to his maneuver (it would have been more dangerous to bail out), and he proceeded to cut off the front of the other guy's board with his fins as he slashed the top of the wave. The other guy should have seen Jeff and realized that the wave belonged to him. Fortunately, aside from a ripped up board, there were no injuries.

Surfing in the 1980s has seen a resurgence of longboarding. Conflict often arises between shortboarders and longboarders because of the differences in the ways the boards work. Many longboarders believe that because they can catch the wave earlier, the wave is theirs. Given today's different types of equipment and styles, this is a selfish attitude which creates bad vibes and tension in the water. It is about time that everyone in the water is regarded as a wave rider with equal opportunity to catch waves.

On the other hand, it must be realized that there are great variations in the levels of ability, aggressiveness, and ego. In many circumstances the size of the ego and aggressiveness out-weighs the surfer's ability. These people are known as "kooks." Kooks can be enormous problems when the surf is small, but when the surf gets big, they usually clear out and go skiing or get sick. The surfer who has lots of ability and experience usually will get more waves than anyone else in the water. He is not necessarily snaking; rather, he just knows his spot and has an innate sense of wave knowledge. This comes with years of surfing and staying in good physical condition. The one rule of etiquette which must always be applied is to use common sense. Don't get in other people's way, but be assertive enough to get waves for yourself.

# Big Saturday: February 1, 1986

After spending most of my day on campus at U.C.S.B., I decided to put my books aside and check the surf. It had been a good winter so far, but we hadn't seen solid waves in two weeks. I meandered down to the cliffs only to find one to three foot bumpy and mushy surf with a chilly winter sea breeze. That morning I had noticed a hefty low pressure system relatively close to our coast, and I had hoped it might pick up throughout the day. I went home and talked my roommate into surfing the junky surf. After that we chowed down and I went to sleep early. I did not sleep well that night, and I kept waking up to what I thought were jet planes starting up at the nearby Santa Barbara airport. The next morning I woke up at about five-thirty to the sound of my dog scratching on the door to get out and do his duties. We walked across the street, and when I stepped up on the curb, all I could see was solid whitewash halfway out to the horizon. I ran back to the house and screamed at my roommate, Gary Olsen, "Wake up! Its huge out front! It's 50 feet!" (I exaggerated.)

"Go away."

"No." I burst into his room and threw off his covers. He hated me then, but his anger didn't last long. We briefly checked it again and without further hesitation grabbed our guns and ran to Campus Point. We both had 7'6" guns shaped by Joe Bark of Palos Verdes. I was trembling at the thought that our boards might be too small. There were only three guys out with many others watching from the cliffs, and the surf was a semi-clean triple overhead plus. Gary has had much big wave experience with about ten trips to Puerto Escondido under his belt, so he charged out first. I soon followed after, praying and mellowing out for five minutes. Gary got out with no problem. Four guys were out now. I charged in and scratched; just as I reached the pit, the biggest wet of the day rolled in and towed me under water almost to the Goleta Pier. I came up blue but laughing. I paddled in and walked back up the point to try again. This time I made it. My first wave lurched and looked as if it could snuff U.C.S.B. Gary shouted, "Go, Bill!" I dropped in, and before I made it to the bottom, a green-brown presence enveloped me. I was truly in the zen-zone as all time stopped. Instinct and reflexes took over as I stood suspended in the rotating room. I escaped as it shouldered off and clam-shelled behind me. I continued screaming for another 200 yards and kicked out before the monster ended in a pounding shore break.

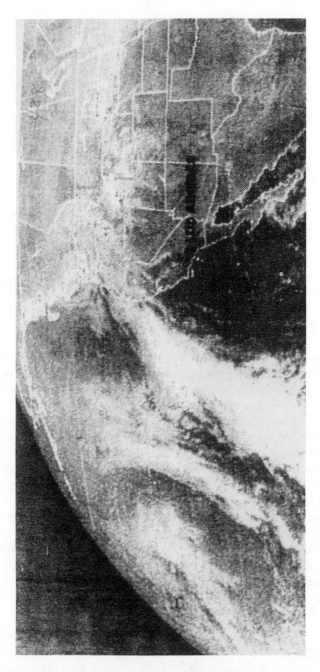

January 28, 1986. This photo shows a lot of activity in the Pacific.
The key here is to watch all three bands of clouds as they progress
in the jet-stream through the week.

January 29. The first band of clouds only brought rain and junky 3-4 foot surf. It is the next band of clouds which holds big surf potential.

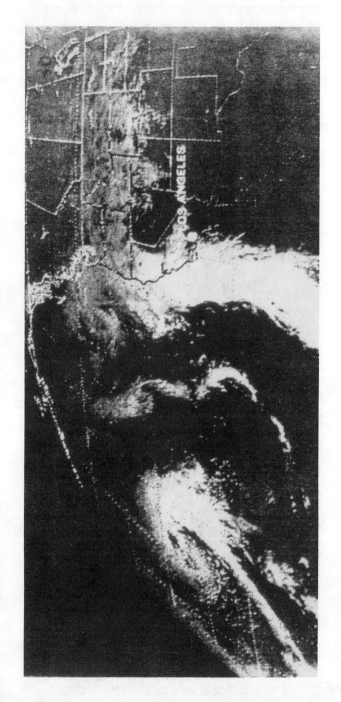

January 30. Some rain and a bit of surf but not gigantic. Continue to watch the spiral of clouds north of Hawaii.

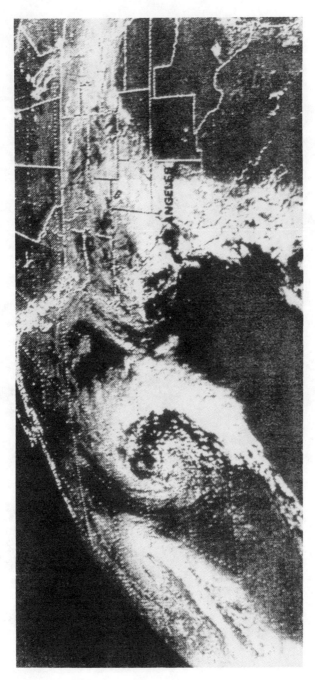

January 31. Still small and junky out, but the second storm will bring a swell. Judging from the January 31 photo, it looks like the swell will hit on Saturday afternoon.

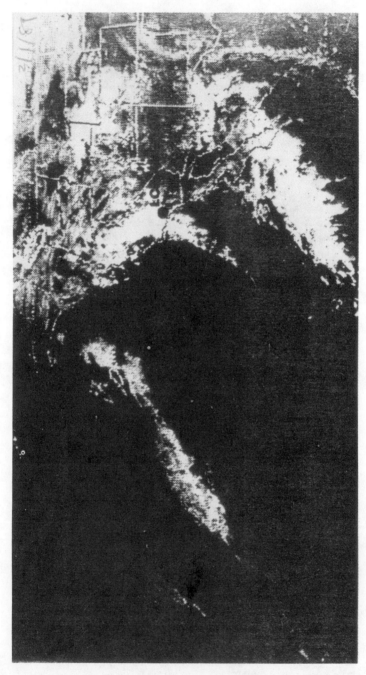

Febuary I.  On Saturday morning the surf hit.  This swell was very
tricky to predict because the storm came ashore much sooner
than the average front.

## Classic Style Contest

In light of modern, aggressive, commercial, profit oriented, overly glamorized, butt waggling surf contests, my friends and I decided to put on a 1960's heavy board competition. The biggest problem we faced was finding a spot that has consistently good surf, easy access, lots of parking, and low crowds. We chose the warm Water Jetties in Carlsbad.

The Warm Water Jetties seemed like a good spot because they have almost all the elements, except for one peculiarity. They are completely missed by south swells. This didn't appear to be a problem because it was only May, which is a little early for a real south to hit. Needless to say, we got a beautiful overhead south swell eight days before the contest. Future competitors were getting pissed at us for picking the only flat spot in San Diego for the contest. Three days before the contest, the surf was still pumping out of the south, and we were beginning to look really stupid. But we knew from the satellite photos that a wind swell from the north was in the making.

As expected, the morning of the contest was greeted with good shaped and head high wind swell peaks; unfortunately, on shore winds accompanied the surf. The wind made the break much gnarlier than it normally is. The surly, untamed peaks mauled more than one contestant. Luckily, the low pressure weather front had passed by ten in the morning, leaving us with sunny skies and cleaner surf. Just before the final heats, we barbequed a giant feast, unloading chicken marinated in Surfer's Choice Marinade. The massive lunch caused all but the final contestants to slip into a deep state of lethargy. While digestion and good times prevailed on the beach, the finalists paddled out for the final event. Author Bill Burke having recently suffered a hernia operation, thought he was going to split at the seams and spill chicken all over the line-up.

When the heat was over, Illima Kalama took first, Bruce Stedge second, and Bill Burke third. Other prizes were given for particular maneuvers like the longest nose ride, worst wipe out, and best pearl. The contest was a success. Author Tom Wegener did not lose face because the study of surfology let him know that the Jetties would break on the day of the contest.

## Blink of an Eye.

In early December, 1987, the National Weather Service issued intense winter storm warnings for the coast of California. Indeed, a severe low was brewing 700 nautical miles west of San Francisco. The media were quick to spread the word of the approaching storm, and for two days the TV news belabored the issue. It was as if all of California would soon be washed away. Surfers everywhere anticipated a giant swell due to the sensational TV

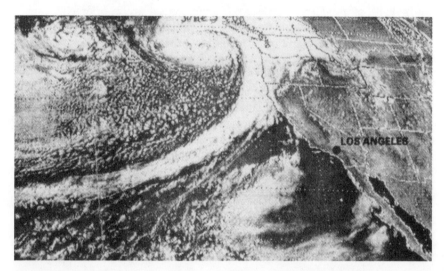

Two days before the contest, a wind swell producing storm fully materialized. But there was still a chance that we would be skunked because the storm was not fully in our swell window. Also, there appeared to be a weak high over us, though the diagrammed map didn't show one.

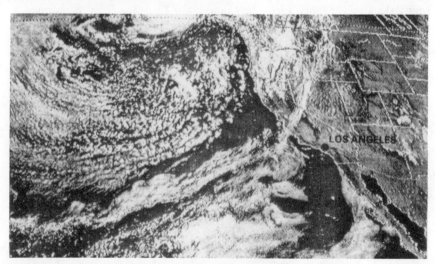

June 4. We became confident that some surf was on the way with this satellite photo because the front had made it into our window. Also, the Pacific was covered with those blotchy wind clouds which always seem to accompany surf.

John Neth cranks a bottom turn.

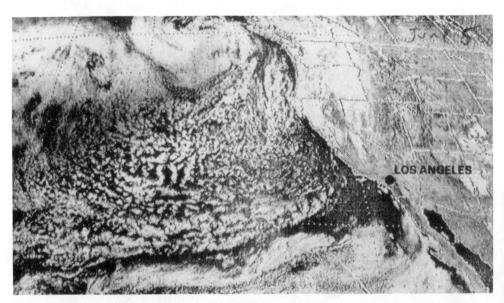

June 5. On the day of the contest, a fun windswell came in, and by 10:00 in the morning it was warm and sunny. Below, John Neth proudly rides to the beach to find that he unanimously won the best pearl prize.

reports. Most big network channels sent reporters to the beach to tell people about the storm but ended up telling them whether or not it was raining. Boy, that's news!

When the storm did hit, it began with a cold, steady rain and some average strength southeast winds. As the night wore on, the winds grew stronger. Outer water marine forecasts called for gale force winds, and small craft warnings were everywhere. This was turning out to be a good storm, but not nearly the Armageddon predicted by Dr. George, Fritz Coleman, or other weather broadcasters. I checked the Torrance beach at Burnout that Monday morning. It was perfect 1 to 2 foot rainy-day long board paradise. I went out for an hour or so and then split to handle my responsibilities. The southeast winds were howling, making offshore chop when I left. Meanwhile, one hundred miles north Santa Barbara harbor was being pummeled by gale force south winds.

My friend, Andy Horton, of Santa Barbara, had anticipated a swell also, so he hit the beach early that Monday morning. Seeing that Santa Barbara surf was wasted by south winds, he headed south for Ventura, which handles south winds better. Sure enough, the swell was hitting Ventura (and had not yet reached the South Bay at Torrance). Andy, his brother and a friend totally scored that morning. The swell was out of the west, but the howling south winds actually broke the swell apart as they traveled down the coast into our waters. This effect made for picture-perfect overhead peaks from Ventura all the way down to Rincon. Andy said he only got out of the water that day to fetch his brother, eat, and take a couple of pictures.

By the time I had returned from handling my responsibilities, it was almost dark. I couldn't believe the dramatic change in size in just four hours. Burnout was solid double overhead, so I raced up and looked at Haggerty's, which was totally flawless and uncrowded. My friend, Chris Schawieker, had been longboarding, but it got huge within one hour so he ran up the street for his 6' 10". I drove home, confident that the surf would be still going the next day.

To my dismay, the next morning produced only 2 to 3 footers. The swell had come and gone in twelve hours....night hours. So the big winners of that storm were those who were out all day, or already out when it hit, because this one came and went with the blink of an eye.

Ventura at its best. Photo Andy Horton.

# About the Authors

Tom Wegener and Bill Burke grew up a block from each other in Palos Verdes Estates, California. Both attended Palos Verdes High School and obtained A. A. degrees from Marymount Palos Verdes Junior College. Tom received a B. A. in Philosophy from the University of California San Diego in 1988 and is currently attending the University of San Diego School of Law. Bill attended the University of California Santa Barbara for one year, and transferred to the University of California Los Angeles where he graduated in 1988 with a B. A. in History. Bill is permanently residing in Santa Barbara.

Tom and Bill have been avid surfers for over twelve years and have surfed the Pacific Coast from Costa Rica to Washington State. In the course of scouring Southern California's coast for the best waves almost every day, they have learned to consistently find and accurately predict the best surf. Tom and Bill enjoy promoting surfing activities, and are also involved in environmental causes.